Praise for
Stories For Boys: A Memoir

With clean vivid descriptions, and ruthless soul-wrenching self-examination, Greg Martin bravely tells a story he never imagined having to tell. The reader is privileged here, to be allowed to watch as he wrestles with his sons, his own belief systems, his urge toward forgiveness and even Walt Whitman. This finely made, deeply felt memoir restores our faith in the power of language and story to make sense of a broken world.

PAM HOUSTON, author of *Contents May Have Shifted*

Stories for Boys is a charming and moving coming-of-age story, its narrator situated in the pivotal position between being his father's son and his sons' father. So refreshing and unique is Martin's treatment of the material that the reader will never mistake this book for its inferior competitors dealing with similar subjects (suicide, latent homosexuality, child abuse). One hopes this is the new wave of memoir: stories of people whose lives are not easily categorized nor dismissed. It is a sweet read.

ANTONYA NELSON, author of *Bound*

Gregory Martin's *Stories for Boys* is a magnetic meditation on what happens when a decades-long lie is brutally revealed. Moving, brave, and unforgettable, this deeply personal book pushes us all further into the light.

CHERYL STRAYED, author of *Wild*

Praise for *Mountain City*

Crystalline ... *Mountain City*, part elegy, part defiance of the elegiac, is the winter view from northern Nevada.

THE NEW YORK TIMES BOOK REVIEW

A crisp elegy to an almost vanished American West.

ENTERTAINMENT WEEKLY

Mountain City celebrates the alternate Western seasons of promise and pessimism, arrival and abandonment. Hardened like the place he sketches against the vagaries of life, Martin writes sensitively without being maudlin, as if pity were something he discovered late in life.

THE DENVER POST

Life in a dying Western town has found its worthy chronicler ... A poetic, tender look at Mountain City, Nevada (population 33), and its denizens ... Martin deftly illuminates the soul and characters behind the crumbling facades."

SEATTLE POST-INTELLIGENCER

Describes the relationships between people ... with precision and care. Highly recommended for all libraries.

LIBRARY JOURNAL

Martin's is a melancholy song, lovely and heartfelt.

Gregory Martin's *Mountain City*, which describes a small community (thirty-three inhabitants when the books opens, thirty-one when it ends) in the mountains of Nevada, is not only a tender and evocative portrait of a place, but also a loving description of Martin's own extended family, who are descended from Cornish miners and Basque sheepherders."

NANCY PEARL, author of *Booklust: Recommended Reading for Every Mood, Moment and Reason*

A keen and witty observer ... Martin shows how frailty is woven into the fabric of relations; he maintains an immediacy that highlights the humanity of his subjects ... gorgeously written, meticulously observed.

In the rural West we're sometimes lucky and get the good books we deserve: *Old Jules, Housekeeping, The Meadow,* and now *Mountain City.* Northern Elko County is its own nation, and this is its sweet, ironic anthem.

WILLIAM KITTREDGE, author of *Hole in the Sky*

Mountain City is at the crossroads of the Western heart – the specific old loved place amid life's inexorable routes to elsewhere. With a jeweler's eye and a descendant's respectful affection, Gregory Martin has caught the cadences of life and lingo in this little Nevada spot that still counts for so much in the American story.

IVAN DOIG, author of *This House of Sky*

...Well-written, sweet, yet unsentimental, telling the shared history of a community that's vanishing.

In prose as clear and full of light as the Western sky, *Mountain City* presents a way of life once common in America, now fading like a sunset. This book simmers with insight and wisdom about family – and a few good jokes, too.

CHRIS OFFUTT, author of *Out of the Woods*

Gregory Martin draws a gently humorous, sensitive sketch of Mountain City and its crusty citizens.

EVAN S. CONNELL, author of *Son of the Morning Star*

Rarely is the story of a place and its people told with such exacting lyricism, clarity and love. Gregory Martin has such a refined eye and ear that this book, composed from mosaic chips of memory, accumulates into one of the most beautiful and significant portraits of an extended family living and dying in the American West that I have ever read.

ALISON HAWTHORNE DEMING, author of *The Edges of the Civilized World*

Gregory Martin has illuminated the lives of the residents of Mountain City, Nevada, like the pages of a medieval manuscript. They glow from within. The book is a classic – simple, elegant, and devastating.

RICHARD SHELTON, author of *Going Back to Bisbee*

In the enchanting microcosm that is *Mountain City*, author Gregory Martin has captured the character of Basques everywhere.

ROBERT LAXALT, author of *Sweet Promised Land*

Library of Congress
Cataloging-in-Publication Data

Martin, Gregory, 1971–
Stories for boys : a memoir /
Gregory Martin.
p. cm.
ISBN 978-0-9834775-8-7 (alk. paper)

1.   Fathers and sons—Biography.
2.   Gay men—Biography.
I. Title.

[HQ755.85.M285 2012]
306.76'620922–DC23
2011039904

Hawthorne Books
& Literary Arts

9   2201 Northeast 23rd Avenue
8   3rd Floor
7   Portland, Oregon 97212
6   hawthornebooks.com
5   *Form:*
4   Adam McIsaac, Bklyn, NY
3
2   Printed in China

Set in Paperback

Photographs contained in *Stories for Boys* are from the author's
personal collection with the following exceptions: p. 23 by Thad-
deus Roan, used by permission; p. 264 by MCA Records, used
by permission; pp. 125, 169, 251 by Library of Congress, used by permission; p. 189 by the Walt Whitman Archive, used by permission;
p. 210 by Dark Horse Media, used by permission; p. 109 by *kewl-
wallpapers.com*, p. 226 by Flickr user *Davidw* and p. 196 by Flickr
user *countylemonade, and* pp. 45, 167, 207, 220, 221 by Wikimedia
Commons used by Creative Commons license.

For my sons, Oliver and Evan.

STORIES
FOR
BOYS

A MEMOIR

GREGORY MARTIN

HAWTHORNE BOOKS & LITERARY ARTS
Portland, Oregon | MMXII

STORIES FOR BOYS

A Phone Call

WE WERE WRESTLING ON THE BED WHEN EVAN FELL OFF headfirst. I saw him go over, his feet and legs rising briefly in the air as he rolled backwards. Then he disappeared. There was an awful thud. I was on all fours; Oliver was sitting on my back. He didn't stop strangling me, but I stopped making my agonal death rattle. Evan gained his feet and shook his head like a wide receiver after getting clotheslined by a linebacker on a route across the middle. Evan was four years old, pale and skinny, his dirty blonde hair sprouting in all directions.

"That's enough," I said. "We've got to stop." Two days in a row was enough. Yesterday, Evan had fallen backwards off the other side of the bed, stopping inches from the floor, his body wedged between the bed and the wall, butt first, his ankles at his ears, like a breech baby deep in the birth canal.

Oliver climbed off my back. He was six. He was both the tallest and the youngest kid in his first grade class.

Evan started to cry. He crawled back on the bed and into my lap. "No, Dad, please," he said. "I won't fall off anymore."

Oliver left the room and came back a minute later with one of those squishy blue gel ice packs from the freezer. He put it on the top of his little brother's head and held it there.

"Thanks, Oliver," Evan said.

"He'll be fine in a minute, Dad," Oliver said. "It's gonna be okay," he said to Evan.

"All right," I said.

"Positions!" Oliver shouted and tossed the ice pack on the floor.

We have positions. I start on my hands and knees in the middle of the bed. Oliver sits on my back with his hands on my shoulders, bucking bronco style. Evan starts directly under my chest, on his back, with his palms on my cheeks. I'm not quite sure how these positions evolved. We have rules, established through trial and error: no punching, slapping, kicking, stomping, tickling, biting, poking in the eyes, nose, or mouth. No shirts. (Yanked shirt collars cause choking.) No nakedness. Oliver and I wrestle in our shorts or jeans. Evan strips down to his Scooby-Doo underpants, which Oliver and I tolerate, though we would prefer he wear shorts or pants. Evan would prefer to wrestle naked, but Oliver and I will not allow it. In the past year, Oliver has discovered modesty; he wants privacy going to the bathroom and changing his clothes. I respect this. It's refreshing. Our house is small – 1,100 square feet. We have only one bathroom. Christine thinks it's perfectly reasonable to floss nakedly while I wipe my ass. I've made it clear to Oliver that I consider him an ally. It does not help that one of the great joys of Evan's life is to take off all his clothes and race around the house the moment we arrive home.

We were still in our start positions when the phone rang. Usually I say, Ready, Set, Go! But Oliver treated the first ring of the phone as a starting gun, spurring my ribs with his bony heels. I twisted sideways, flipped him onto his back and squashed him like a bug with my chest. The air went whoosh out of his lungs. Christine came in the bedroom with a worried look on her face.

"It's your mom," she said. "She's really upset."

This was not good. My mother is a stoic Nevadan. Her hero is John Wayne. (Really. There is a poster of the young Duke in her office – a three foot high close-up of his face. He's wearing a white ten-gallon cowboy hat.) I can count on one hand the number of times she's mentioned the word bipolar, a disorder she's suffered from since she was a teenager. She treated her stage

3-c ovarian cancer, the surgery that removed her uterus, much of her bladder and colon, and the eight rounds of chemotherapy that followed, like a series of unpleasant dental procedures. Oliver grabbed my throat. Evan poked his finger up my nose. I stood up and the boys fell off me, back on the bed, shouting protests. I took the phone into the guest bedroom. I thought then that my mother's cancer had come back. Or that my cousin's breast cancer had come back. Or my grandmother – my father's mother – had died. She was eighty-eight, frail and declining, had Alzheimer's, and lived in a nursing home in Georgia.

"Your father tried to kill himself," she said.

Two Revelations

ON THURSDAY, MAY 3RD, 2007, AT ABOUT SIX IN THE evening, in Spokane, Washington, my mother and father had a fierce argument. Fights and conflict were rare for them, and never lasted long. They'd been married thirty-nine years. They had a happy marriage. My father said, "If you want me to go, then I'll really go." He went upstairs. A few minutes later, my mother followed. She found him sitting on the end of their bed, his eyes unfocused, his head and shoulders sagging. "What did you do?" she shouted. "I took some pills," my father answered. "You won't have to worry about me anymore." My mother went into the bathroom. All the bottles from the medicine cabinet, a pharmacy's worth of drugs including the Ativan and Trazodone my mother took for bipolar disorder, were out and open and empty on the counter. She called 911.

The last thing my father ever wanted was to be a character in a melodrama. He did not want to step on stage at sixty-six, his hair gray, a small paunch over his belt, and play the tragic lead. He wanted to drink Coca-cola and watch Jeopardy! and listen to The Kingston Trio, to bowl and play cribbage with my mother, to read science fiction novels and watch movies with explosions, to work as a speech pathologist in a nursing home, helping the elderly to speak again and swallow soft foods like yogurt and rice pudding.

Two days later, on the fifth floor of the psychiatric ICU of Spokane's Sacred Heart Hospital, after my father had spent thirty-six hours in a coma on a ventilator, the intubation tube was removed from his throat. His head back on his pillow, his eyes closed, his face pale, he slowly regained consciousness. He recognized me as I gripped his hand, touched his forehead. The agony etched on his wrinkled face was clear. He did not want to be alive.

For hours, my father would not speak. Tears leaked slowly from his eyes.

For the past two days, my mother had refused to tell me why he had done this. "Your father will have to tell you himself." She could hardly look at me. She said this each time I asked, and I asked more than a few times. She said this even in the first hours after his suicide attempt, when it wasn't clear if he'd pull through, as if she was willing to let him take his reasons to the grave.

I told my father I loved him, and he mouthed the words, "You won't."

My father told me two things that day, two revelations which I had never once suspected. He told me that for ten years, from the time he was four until he was fourteen, his father had molested him. His voice broke as he said this. He hesitated and looked wildly about the room. I moved toward him. My father held up his hand. "I'm not done." He then said that he'd been having anonymous affairs for as long as he and my mother had been married – for thirty-nine years. All of these affairs were with men. He was gay. My father cried as he spoke. I cried with him. I told him I was grateful he was alive.

For the next half hour or so, I sat with my father beside his bed. Or my mother sat at his side, talking to him in a quiet voice and holding his hand and stroking his thin, gray hair. Or she stood at the edge of the room, her mouth in a tight line, her arms crossed, her eyes far away.

Windows

IT IS SUMMER AND DUSK AND MY FATHER IS SEVEN YEARS old. He lives with his mother and sisters in a small apartment with a porch facing the street and an unfenced backyard. The night is hot and humid and the windows are open, the air heavy with the smell of Virginia's James River and of coal. My father is reading a Donald Duck comic in the bedroom he shares with his two sisters, teenagers and out somewhere. He sits at the edge of the bed, still dressed in shorts and shirtsleeves, his hair neatly combed. His mother sits at the table in the kitchen: maybe she is paying bills or flipping through the newspaper looking for sales or looking out the window at the coming dark. She works a sixty-hour week at the Newport News shipyard as a drafting technician. She walks to work each day to save the twenty cents of bus fare so her children will have lunch money for school. From the alley, my father hears pebbles crunching beneath tires, an engine downshifting, the familiar grind of brakes. A car door opens and closes. Then his father is shouting. Awful things – about his mother, about his sisters, about him. My father doesn't need to look out the window to see the drunken sneer on his father's face. He knows his father will not leave until one of the neighbors calls the police. The neighbors' windows are open, every one, every single window, and shame quickens in my father's gut.

Other times his father lets the car idle in the alley while he gets out, stands quietly, and smokes a cigarette. He lingers there in silence for ten minutes, twenty minutes, an hour, and my father feels the horrible pull of his father's gravity like the moon's on tidewater.

MY FATHER TOLD me this story late at night in the psychiatric ICU as I willed myself to stay awake on my cot. He was on suicide watch. We had long since turned out the lights. I still didn't trust that he wouldn't try to kill himself. I kept having dark premonitions. I'd heard him stir in his bed and asked him what he was thinking. The blinds to the locked windows of our fifth-floor room were open wide.

Later that night I startled awake. My father was out of bed. It was sometime past midnight. The room had a bathroom, and he'd gone inside and shut the door. He was in there a long time. Too long. I waited and waited. I could feel my pulse throbbing in my neck. Finally I got up and went over and banged hard on the metal door with the side of my fist.

"What? What?" my father shouted.

I let out a gasp. I'd been holding my breath. I tried the door. It was unlocked. I opened it. My father was sitting on the toilet in his gown.

It took me a few moments to speak. My father looked at me. His face was covered in gray stubble. The light in the bathroom was bright. His eyes were wet and glistening. He could not control the movements of his mouth.

"I'm sorry," I said. "You were in here so long. I thought – "

He met my eyes and shook his head but couldn't speak.

"Come on, Dad," I said, and I helped him up off the toilet, and I held him by the arm and he put his hand on my shoulder. I guided him through the near dark over to the hospital bed and pulled the thin, white cotton blanket up over his chest.

I had been a father, myself, for almost seven years. But I did not tell him in a soft, reassuring voice that everything would be okay.

Too Many Choices

THAT SUNDAY AFTERNOON, MY FATHER ASKED IF HE could have fried chicken for dinner, from Albertson's, with potato salad and baked beans. Here was the father, and the appetite, I knew. As soon as he said it, I had the same craving.

Twenty minutes later, my mother and I were in the Albertson's parking lot. It was a hot day, and we were about to enter the automatic sliding glass doors and the air conditioning, when my mother stopped, turned to me and said, "Your father told me he's been with more than one thousand men. He goes to High Bridge Park, on the other side of town. He seemed relieved to

give me a number, an estimate. Why would he tell me that? Why would he say that to me?"

I didn't know. I felt hollow. I could not imagine the depth of grief my mother must have been feeling in that moment.

We went into the store and bought fried chicken and home fries, baked beans, coleslaw, and potato salad. We bought Cokes for my father and me and for my older brother, Chris, who'd flown in from Maryland. My mother stood in front of the refrigerator case, staring at the iced teas. Lipton, Snapple, AriZona, Nestea. Strawberry, Raspberry, Brisk Lemon, Lime, Diet Peach, Cactus, Very Cherry. She seemed paralyzed. "There shouldn't be so many choices," she said.

The next day, my father vowed that he was no longer a danger to himself and so was discharged from the hospital. On the way home, in the car, my mother leaned forward from her place in the back seat and said to him, "I want you to move out." I was driving. My father was in the passenger seat. Chris was in the back seat beside my mother. We were all wearing our seat belts. My father's expression went from shocked, to bereft, to sinister. He turned to look at my mother.

I said, "Don't look at her like that." I had never used this tone of voice with my father in my life.

My father ignored me. He said to my mother, "That's not what we talked about."

"I said I didn't know," she said quietly. " I know now."

I stopped at a red light. It was a beautiful sunny day in Spokane, the trees leafed out and green, the sharp afternoon light bursting through the canopy. My father seemed to think that because he'd tried to kill himself, and survived, that this somehow proved how much he'd never wanted to hurt my mother, proved how much it hurt him to hurt her, proved how much he loved her, a love that had nothing to do with him being gay, and so she could not make him leave, or divorce him. Not now.

My mother stared back. Her eyes did not leave his. She said, "You need to be gone by tomorrow."

My father slept that night in the guest bedroom. He spent Tuesday and Wednesday with Chris in a hotel. My mother left for work early in the morning, and my father came back to the house from the hotel, and my brother and I helped him pack boxes and rent the U-Haul. My father had moved many times before, but he seemed to have forgotten how the process worked. My brother and I passed him carrying boxes, while he stood in the kitchen, the bedroom, the basement, the driveway, staring into the middle distance. Figuring out how everything fit in the truck was not nearly as enjoyable as usual.

On Thursday, Chris and I helped our father move into a cheap apartment across town. It was the first apartment we looked at. As we pulled into the parking lot that morning, I thought of the apartment my father grew up in, near the railroad tracks in Newport News. We walked through the empty rooms with beige carpet and bare white walls. My father turned to the manager, an older lady with a smoker's cough, white hair, and a Mickey Mouse t-shirt, and he said, "Okay. I'll take it." We walked outside and down the steps. In the courtyard, a little boy about Evan's age was having lunch by himself at a picnic table chained to a tree.

Resilience

THE SUNDAY AFTER MY FATHER WAS DISCHARGED FROM the hospital happened to be Mother's Day. I was still in Spokane. My brother had flown back to Maryland the day before. I missed Christine and the boys, but whatever had been vital and urgent in my daily life in Albuquerque felt suspended, as if my father had died, as if he'd committed rather than attempted suicide.

I felt shattered. Late at night on the phone, I talked and talked to Christine, and she listened. Christine is a talented listener. Unlike me, she doesn't interrupt with highly workable solutions, with suggestions and advice, with interpretations of significance. She just let me talk. I didn't have to make sense of anything.

Christine said, "I'm so sorry." And, "I wish I could be there with you." And, "You must be so sad."

For seven years, my life had been dominated by fatherhood. I was not used to thinking of myself as a son. I was not used to thinking of myself as deceived. I was not used to thinking much about my father at all. When I thought of my parents – no, when I worried about my parents – I worried about my mother's ovarian cancer and her chemotherapy, or I worried about whether or not my father was making sure that my mother was taking her bipolar medication. I needed my father to keep his eye on things. It never once occurred to me that my mother might need to keep a closer eye on him.

I stayed in Spokane for nearly two weeks. I didn't feel ready

to leave my mother on her own. Another way to say this is that I needed her to not be alone because I couldn't bear the sadness she had to bear.

MY MOTHER AND father loved each other. Their love was unferocious, grudgeless, without jealousy or tyranny, delirium or disdain. It was playful, gentle. A love hard to find in books. It was rooted in an abiding friendship and a mutual, lifelong desire for each other's company. They often abandoned me to friends and neighbors and went, of all places, to garage sales and auctions. Their zeal for garage sales and auctions was matched by many things, like bowling, like playing cribbage or two-handed pinochle late into the evening. They went for walks; they read books side by side for hours upon hours.

When I was a child, we'd gather in the living room, and my father would play folk songs on the guitar, and we'd all sing. "Michael Row Your Boat Ashore" and "Blowing in the Wind" and "Five Hundred Miles" and "Hard Times Come Again No More." My father's voice was, and still is, deep and soulful. My mother cannot carry a tune. She has – and she will freely admit this – a terrible singing voice. All through my childhood, my mother's voice threatened to pull each of us away from the melody. The quality of her singing voice was often acknowledged. My mother sang anyway, gleefully, and I'm guessing now that my father loved her even more for this. Of course he did. Sometimes at the end of a song, my mother said, "God hears my true voice." And my father would say, "Of course he does." Or, "He must." Or, "I hear it, too."

These days, the implicit code is that parents put their love of their children first, before their love for one another, and only controversial parents are willing to declare that they put their love for their spouses first. When I was growing up, I unconsciously understood that my parents' love for each other was always first, and then came their love for their children. I did not question this. I had no reason to question it. Nothing seemed wrong.

NINE DAYS AFTER my father attempted suicide, my mother and I went bowling. She did not want to stay at home, perfecting her dignity and resilience. She was sixty-seven. Her hair was more gray and white than black and more thin since it had grown back after the chemotherapy four years earlier. She had a red scar down the middle of her nose from the surgery to remove skin cancer a few years before that. Both cancers were in remission. She worked full time as a university dean. She walked three miles a day. She ate steel-cut oatmeal with fresh fruit for breakfast. She ate a sweet potato with cinnamon for lunch. She drank her English breakfast tea with a splash of sweetened, condensed milk. She'd grown up in a small town in northern Nevada, and as a young woman was accomplished with a rifle and one winter even ran a trap-line and sold beaver and mink and fox pelts, but now she did yoga once a week. She bowled on teams in two different leagues. Summer league would be starting in a few weeks, and she needed to practice.

When I was a boy growing up in Nebraska, my mother and I bowled together in the Cornstalk and Kernel league. We cleaned up; we took first place several years running. This may be mythmaking, but in my memory, one year we each had high average and high score in our respective parent/child categories.

In May of each year, my mother and her sister, my aunt Di, travel to a different mid-sized city – Topeka, Oklahoma City, Reno – bowling in the Senior U.S. Nationals. Every October, they bowl in the World Senior Games in St. George, in southern

Utah. My mother doesn't rattle. She has uncanny consistency.
Her address and approach are always the same – three steps, a
slight hop, her backswing in a single plane, her knee bent low
at release, her follow-through as if she were about to shake your
hand. She throws the same first ball every time. One year, at
Nationals, she and her doubles partner took second place out of
7,322 other doubles teams.

But on this particular day, my mother was off her mark.
She threw bedpost splits and baby splits. She kept hitting the
Brooklyn side of the headpin. Her ball drifted toward the gutter
as if drawn by a magnet. If she knocked down eight pins, one of
the remaining pins was hidden, a sleeper. She threw open frame
after open frame. No strikes, no spares. All this, despite having
her own monogrammed ball, her own shoes, her own wrist
brace and powder and towel. I was wearing worn-out red and
green rental shoes. The thumbhole of my rental ball was too
loose. But I struck the pocket flush. I threw strike after strike. It
was my day. I had great action, the pins flying and mixing. The
first two games weren't even competitive. My mother bowled
more than thirty pins below her average. I didn't have an average –
I hadn't bowled in a few years – but if I bowled like this all the
time, I could quit my job as a teacher and join the tour. I could
be on ESPN2.

My mother said, "Does Christine have any idea about the
secret life you've been leading at Holiday Bowl?"

I shook my head but didn't laugh. I didn't turn to look at her.
I was looking down the shiny lane at the pins, set up in their
orderly configuration. I had always appreciated my mother's
black humor, but I wasn't ready to hear it just then. I didn't want
to think about my father. I didn't want to think at all. This is
something I can do, something I've always been able to do. Put
things away – events, feelings – put them far from my mind and
my heart.

I wanted to throw a strike, and I did. I walked back to take
my seat. "Christine has no idea," I said.

The third game was closer. I'd been trying to throw strikes, but with my second ball, I sandbagged a few of the spares. I wanted to at least make it close, but at the same time, I didn't want my mother to know. She wouldn't like that. My mother was the only person I knew who hated losing more than I did – at anything, it didn't matter what, pinochle, horseshoes, you name it – but she wanted to win fair and square. She was fierce about fairness. On my last ball, for a spare in the tenth frame, I guttered a makeable leave. I lost by three pins.

My mother said, "You did that on purpose."

I thought I would lie, but found that I couldn't. "I did. Yes."

"I wouldn't have done that," my mother said fiercely. Seriousness was all over her face. "I would have beat you."

"I know."

Don't Go There

THE NEXT DAY, I DROVE OVER TO MY FATHER'S CHEAP apartment. My father had been there for five days. Unopened boxes were everywhere. I told him it was time to unpack. He shrugged. He stood there with his hands at his sides, watching me look around, taking in this new life. There was nowhere for him to sit down. No La-Z-Boy recliner with its worn, wooden handle. No sofa. Two folding chairs leaned against the wall.

I found his small pocketknife on the counter next to his keys and started cutting open boxes. One of the first things I unwrapped from the crumpled newspaper was a glass ashtray. I held it in my hand; it was heavy. I was baffled.

My father saw me sitting there, cross-legged on the beige carpet, holding the ashtray. He said, "I smoke."

I'd thought my father had given up smoking when I was six or seven, after he got tired of me taking his cartons from the refrigerator and burying them at the bottom of the neighbor's trash. I stared at him. Gray and white hair sprouted from the v–neck of his white t-shirt. He wore jeans and was in his bare feet. There was nothing unusual about this. My father was not a man who wore golf shirts and khakis on the weekends. But he looked disheveled to me now. I had the sense that if I had not been there he'd lay back down on the unmade bed and stare at the ceiling. He was still standing by the door.

"I tried to quit I don't know how many times. But I never really did."

My father has severe asthma and chronic bronchitis.
I decided to name my feelings, something Christine and I were
trying to teach the boys to do at home. But instead of saying
"I'm angry," I said "I feel like throwing this at your head."

My father thought about this. He went over and started un-
folding the card table which would now be his dining room
table. Then he said, "You've always had good aim." He didn't look
up. He took paperbacks from another box and stacked them in
a pile against the wall. He didn't have a bookshelf.

All morning I vacillated between feeling nauseated with
sadness and disbelief and losing myself in the task at hand and
making small comments like, "Where do you want this?" and
opening the window and saying, "It's a really nice day." Because
it was. It was another warm, early summer day in Spokane.
My father and I settled into the work of unpacking, arranging his
apartment. We set up his modular office furniture in the spare
bedroom. We talked about what he'd need to do to set up his
internet connection.

I hate this feeling—the lapsing into normalcy when things
are anything but normal. I wonder if other people despise it as
much as I do. Everything about the big picture is wrong, and I'm
making turkey sandwiches on white bread with mayo and mus-
tard and iceberg lettuce for my father and me for lunch, and my
mouth is watering, and we sit down at the card table, on folding
chairs, and eat, and for a few moments, this feels as familiar
and normal and seemingly uneventful as any other turkey sandwich I've eaten with my father over the years. My father is an
easy man to eat lunch with; he's agreeable, warm, quick to laugh,
skilled at finding common ground, good at asking the kinds of
questions that draw people out and get them to talk about things
that matter to them. My father was asking me about the boys'
summer plans, and I was talking about swim team and art camp,
and it was almost as if I'd forgotten how awful things were. I was
no longer trying to separate what was done to my father when
he was a boy, when he was an innocent, from what my father did

to my mother, for nearly forty years, when he was culpable, accountable. I'd stopped trying to untangle my confused sympathies, and so when my father said, "It's too bad we don't have potato chips," I added, without thinking, "Christine would cut up an apple. We don't get to have potato chips at lunch."

I hate this. I prefer no break, no distraction, from misery. I want what Jamaica Kincaid calls a "prolonged visit to the bile duct."

I did not want to tell my father about Oliver's and Evan's summer plans. I wanted to rail and shout, "I do not want to be here! How is this even possible that I'm unpacking boxes in this cheap apartment? This isn't fair. Why do I have to do this? What the hell has happened? How did you suddenly become a complete mystery? Who are you?" But no. I was not vigilant enough. My father said, "But this turkey sandwich still hits the spot," and without thinking, I said, "Definitely."

Spending time with my father in those first two weeks after he attempted suicide, I realized how truly talented he was at the pretense of normalcy. His ability to withstand silences without awkwardness, to deflect emotionally-loaded questions with mild evasions, was Olympian. It was as if he had trained his entire life for this event.

At one point, I asked him if he thought his mom (whom we called MomMom), ever suspected that he was gay when he was a teenager. "No. She had no idea." My father was attaching the cables of the DVD to the TV. "I think I might get DirecTV. Do you know anything about that?"

"No. Do you think your sisters ever suspected anything?"

"No. If I get DirecTV, then I can tape *Jeopardy!*. Well, it doesn't really tape it, because you don't have to rewind. It would just store it for you. I've wanted to do that for a while, but your mother didn't think it was worth the expense. When we get the phone line connected and the internet up and running, that's something I'm going to look into."

The day passed. My father's cheap apartment looked less and less bare and more like an inhabited place of exile.

WE WENT OUT to dinner at Perkins. My father ordered chicken fried steak in a thick gravy. I had a cheeseburger and fries. We were quiet together for several minutes.

Finally I said, "How did you sleep last night?"

"Terribly. You want to know something?"

"What?"

"If your brother hadn't been with me those first two nights at the hotel, I would have gone to the park."

My brother had flown back to Maryland nearly a week before. I did and did not want to know the answer to the question I then asked. "Did you go there, to the park, last night?"

I saw what I took to be fear flash across my father's face. Then he set his jaw and narrowed his eyes, as if I had just broken some unspoken agreement the two of us had always shared, as if, according to the rules, we could imply such things but not state them outright. "I don't want to answer that," he said and looked away, out the window, to the traffic headed north on Division Street, the cars with their lights on in the dusk.

"There's no reason to lie anymore," I said.

He thought about this for a while. I could almost see him struggling against the inertia of chronic untruthfulness. Then he said angrily, "Okay. Well then, yes. Yes, I did. I went there last night."

Spokesman Review Metro Edition

PLAGUE IN THE PARK

Those trying to enjoy creek, river areas find debris repulsive

BYLINE: JoNel Aleccia, Staff writer

SECTION: A; Pg. 1

There's nothing new about the sexual detritus left in the bushes at Spokane's High Bridge Park.

Discarded underwear, empty lubrication packets and used condoms are only the most visible evidence of public sex acts occurring regularly at the 200-acre city site. In fact, almost no one – from City Council members and park managers to health officials and police officers – disputes that the area has been notorious for lewd activity for years, even decades.

"It's just kind of one of those knowns in Spok ane," said Spokane Police Officer Jennifer DeRuwe.

But that explanation doesn't sit well with Ruby La Fleur, 62, a longtime neighbor who said she's worried about the health effects of the sordid litter – and tired of the people who leave it behind.

"I have grandkids up here," said La Fleur, who lives just above the park at the confluence of the Spokane River and Latah Creek.

"I don't want them walking through the bushes, saying 'Grandma Ruby, what's that toilet paper? What are those rubber gloves for? What are those pictures?'"

And La Fleur is not alone. Spokane police have been fielding an increasing number of complaints about the area of High Bridge Park and nearby People's Park, said DeRuwe.

In the past five years, the department has recorded 27 calls for service involving lewd conduct and 30 calls about suspicious people in vehicles, said Cpl. Tom Lee, police information officer.

Some of those calls have led to arrests, including six in June for lewd conduct.

But that's only a fraction of the actual illegal behavior that goes on, said La Fleur and a young city parks employee who has been assigned to the area this summer.

In the nearly two months that he's worked in the park, the 22-year-old caretaker says he has been propositioned by men seeking homosexual sex and witnessed evidence of public sexual activity.

The young man, who asked not to be identified because of fear about his safety, said he has begun warning unwary visitors attracted by the new disc golf course and a new bike trail link.

"I tell them, 'Don't let your kids go in there.'"

Propensities

I DIDN'T KNOW HOW TO RECONCILE MY FATHER'S "LEWD conduct" with the man I thought I knew. My father? 1,000 men? What was I supposed to call that? Desire gone haywire, its idle set too high? Compulsion? Obsession? Addiction? Whatever it was called, I had to find some way to separate my father's authentic sexuality from what seemed like absurdity and squalor.

My father didn't go to a public park late at night for anonymous sex nine days after he tried to kill himself because he was seeking existential healing. He went for a moment of relief. What I wished, then, was that I didn't know this about him, because this knowledge pained and embarrassed me. I did not want to accommodate it, integrate it somehow into my notions of family and father. I did not want to be associated with such sordid desperation. I felt tainted, compromised, ashamed. I was this man's son?

But I refused to pursue these thoughts then, in those first few weeks and months. I refused to admit these things to myself, to descend to that level of emotional honesty, because such acknowledgements ran contrary to my notion of myself as open, understanding, compassionate. These were not the feelings of the person I thought myself to be.

The father I'd always known was grounded, affable, calm. But this man was driven by a carnal appetite I couldn't comprehend. I'd always assumed that my father's inner life was a mirror of his outer life. This man's inner life was a cauldron, a maelstrom.

Yes, his homosexuality was a shock. But the real, lasting shock is that unquenchable desire that I never, not once, had any intimation or sense of—that he was so profoundly different from the man I thought I knew. 1,000 men. The self-loathing and shame and dark, inner loneliness; the cathartic, self-flagellation that must accompany the confession of such a number.

Subject: **RE: checking in**

Date: Wed, 30 May 2007

Hi Greg,

Sorry about taking so long to reply to your email. I didn't have internet service until last week and I've gotten so little email over the past few years that I really didn't even think to check until the other night and it was too late to give a reply the thought I thought appropriate.

I am doing OK as far as I know. I don't break down into a ball of mush anymore and that's an improvement. I think a lot about your Mom and I miss her a great deal. The divorce papers have been filled and will probably be final on Sept. 20. I, quite frankly, look forward to having an excuse to call Mom just to talk to her for a while. Otherwise, I'm doing OK at work and getting the apartment settled. This weekend, I bought a new sofa and side chair as well as some living room tables. They won't be delivered for about 4 weeks.

As to who I really am, I'm still and always will be the same person you've known all your life, except that now you know the one part of my life that I've only shared with a Priest in confession before. You have lost an image of me once thought to be carved in stone and it must be difficult to imagine what might eventually replace it.

About your questions: Your mother and I were raised in a different atmosphere, both from each other and from the era in which you were raised. We didn't talk about such things openly, especially in the South. It never occurred to me to bring it up, much less admit to it. It was enough that I felt so much hate for my father because of what he did to me and the rest of my family. There was then, as there is now a great deal of shame attached to sexual abuse by a family member, especially one's own father. The difference now is that children are encouraged to talk to a responsible person in literally dozens of places in their environment, TV, radio, school, church, camp, etc. This was never the case when I grew up. I don't know what else to say, except that it was a different time.

Even though I know your papers, work, and family take up a great deal of your time, I hope this kind of dialogue can continue as much as you are able. I promise to check my email more often. Please give Christine and the boys a kiss and a hug for me and tell them I love you all very much.

Dad

The Mayor

MY NICKNAME AT THE PARK IN OUR NEIGHBORHOOD IS "The Mayor." It's earned. I play the part. I know the names of all the parents, the toddlers, all the babies in the Baby Bjorns. I know the names of most of the dogs. I remember the names of visiting grandparents and where they're from. I don't have to try. I can talk sports or charter schools, sleep-deprivation or kitchen remodel while at the same time making sure the boys aren't pouring sand on a baby's head, peeing in the bushes with their shorts and underpants at their ankles, or chasing a ball into the street. I have a talent for benign neglect. At the park, when someone asks how I'm doing, I give them an update, generally upbeat, and follow up with my own questions. I tell corny jokes. Some of the best involve Bascos – people who share my Basque heritage. Here's one.

> Five Bascos are in a boat and they have six cigarettes but no lighter. So they decide to throw one of the cigarettes overboard to make the boat a cigarette lighter.

All my life, I had prided myself on my emotional stability, my lack of angst. I took credit for my temperament the way one might take credit for a pleasant smile which never required orthodontic intervention. I didn't need to always "process." The overexamined life was not worth living. I believed in myself. I believed that, with hard work, good things would happen. I said things like, "You make your own luck." I suffered from a classic

case of what psychologists call "optimism bias," believing that I was far more competent and in control than I actually was.

But that summer after my father attempted suicide, I stopped bantering. I cut the corny jokes from my stump speech. I found myself processing, strangely, with my constituents.

"Hey, it's the Mayor, how are you?"

I'd wait for Oliver and Evan to run over to the swings or the playground structure. Then I'd say, "Well, not so good, really."

"Oh."

"Yeah, my father tried to kill himself. He's gay. He was molested as a child."

A look of confusion and then horror would come over their face, followed by a long awkward silence. "Wow. That's hard. I'm really sorry."

We'd stand there for a while, looking at our feet, then at the kids on the playground having fun. After an excruciating twenty more seconds or so, one of us would walk off in the direction of our children. It was embarrassing. Aside from my easily stored mayoral data set, I did not know these parents well. My closest friends had heard about what had happened from Christine. It was a relief that they knew and I didn't have to explain anything. Most offered brief, non-specific consolations, but didn't attempt to draw me out. I wandered the periphery of our summer gatherings. A few friends from my past who lived far away listened on the phone while I talked and talked. But at the park, with these playground acquaintances, I couldn't help myself. I couldn't just go through the motions. I must have had a feral look in my eyes, like I might start howling any moment.

These odd conversations happened a few times – let's say five times – over the course of a couple weeks, and it came to me that I was delivering these kind, well-meaning people an emotional sucker punch. *You want to know how I am? I'll tell you how I am.* Why was I doing this? I didn't know, and so I asked Robert, the wise, bearded counselor I'd started seeing, what he thought. Robert was a grandfather who wore sweater vests like Mr. Rogers, but he didn't counsel like Mr. Rogers.

Robert did not say things like, "Why don't *you* tell me what you think first?" I'd ask him a question, and he'd answer, often at considerable length, effortlessly articulate for minutes at a time. He spoke in paragraphs with compelling topic sentences. He would get fired up. He'd swear for emphasis like a character in a David Mamet play. I appreciated this. He couldn't talk long enough as far as I was concerned.

For years, I'd held the progressive, unjudgmental belief that counseling was a very good thing for certain people – people who didn't quite have their act together or who were temperamentally more like Woody Allen, as himself, in whatever movie. I was more like Tommy Lee Jones, as the Texas Ranger Woodrow F. Call, in the mini-series version of *Lonesome Dove*. Life was hard, not unlike a cattle drive from Texas to Montana in the last days of the Old West, but you weathered it as best you could.

But then one night the summer after my father attempted suicide, I was in bed again before dinner, staring at the ceiling, when Oliver came in and crawled under the covers with me. I was in my red plaid flannel pajamas; he was in shorts and his Run-for-the-Zoo t-shirt. He rubbed my head, not saying anything. Oliver didn't know about his grandpa's suicide attempt or his grandparents' divorce. We hadn't told him. He didn't know why I was so sad. After maybe three minutes, Oliver left and came back. He set a glass of water and an apple on the bedside table, next to the lamp. "Try to get some rest, Dad. You'll feel better tomorrow." He climbed back on the bed and kissed my cheek. He stayed with me for what seemed like a long time, five minutes or more. Then he patted my head and went off to play with his toys.

I didn't want Oliver bringing me any more apples. The sons of Texas Rangers don't bring their depressed fathers apples in bed.

Robert leaned forward in his swivel chair. He said, "Maybe you don't have to be so magnanimous all the time. Maybe you just need to let your Dad have it, the full dose of anger and resentment."

"I don't want to push him over the edge."

"Do you know that if your father had committed suicide, Oliver and Evan would be eight times more likely to commit suicide themselves? They would jump from one statistical category to another, just like that. One third of the insurance companies in America would not offer them life insurance. Doesn't that make you just a little angry? Suicide is the worst How Dare You situation of all, the most selfish, the most egregious. Your father doesn't need your gentle acceptance. That's the last thing he needs. He needs forgiveness, yes. But he hasn't earned it. He needs to feel your full sense of betrayal and anger. Anytime your father disappoints you – doesn't even call on Oliver's birthday or send a card or get him a present, to take the most recent example, that's a How Dare You situation. How *dare* you? How could you fail to even acknowledge your grandson's birthday, after all you've done?

"Father's Day is coming up, you know. Your low-grade depression, your inability to concentrate, your lack of optimism, these weird interactions with people at the park – that's his gift to you. His inevitable ineptitude at keeping his secret has affected everyone who loves him. Some aspect of their lives is fucked up because of him. He needs your disapproval and your anger, your dissatisfaction and outrage. That might be the most valuable Father's Day gift you can give him."

Robert looked at me.

"Anger," I said.

"Yeah," Robert said. "Think about it."

"Happy Father's Day," I said.

"Exactly."

Don't Ask, Don't Tell

MY FATHER GREW UP BELIEVING HE'D GRADUATE FROM high school and join the army or navy. His father had been in the merchant marines and worked as a civilian machinist in the Newport News shipyards. The Army's Fort Eustis was a fifteen minute drive from where my father lived. His two older sisters had each, as teenagers, married men stationed there. One brother-in-law, my uncle Dennis, became a Colonel. The other, my uncle Chuck, became a Major General; he was the program manager for both the Black Hawk and the Apache attack helicopter programs, and was later commanding general at Aberdeen Proving Ground.

But when my father tried to enlist after high school, he was found to have bilateral cataracts. He was blind in bright sunlight. He would not be able to defend himself in all battle situations. He was turned away. He went to college at Virginia Tech instead, where he majored in political science and played folk guitar at house parties and met my mother. But there was something my mother did not think to ask him, and there was something my father did not tell.

A Plot with a Mystery

THE MORNING AFTER MY FATHER WOKE FROM HIS COMA, Oliver and Evan wrote and illustrated get well cards and put them in the mailbox down by the sidewalk, where they fought over who got to lift up the red flag. These cards did not say, *Get well soon, Grandpa, how could you do this, you, you, you … idiot.* These cards were merely sweet and contextually heartbreaking. The boys knew only that their grandpa had been sick and I'd gone to visit him, and he was getting better.

In the first week in July, my mother flew to Albuquerque to visit. The day before she came, Christine and I decided we had to tell the boys something. Granny was coming to stay with us, but Grandpa wasn't? Why? So that night at dinner, we told the boys that Granny and Grandpa had divorced. Sometimes people just can't find a way to love each other anymore. Sometimes they just need to be apart. It doesn't mean they hate each other. It just means they want to live alone now.

This account failed to satisfy them. Because it didn't make any sense. It wasn't quite the truth, and it was a lousy story, mired in vagueness and abstraction. Oliver and Evan had visited Granny's and Grandpa's house plenty of times – Granny and Grandpa had visited our house plenty of times – and nothing had ever been wrong. For a few moments – for three or four seconds – Oliver and Evan made these counter-arguments with their eyes.

Then Evan wailed like he'd been stabbed. Oliver set his jaw and looked out the window.

We told them not to worry. This would not happen to Mommy and Daddy. Never worry about that. Mommy and Daddy loved each other, and we were going to spend our whole lives together. But of course they were worried. We could see it in their eyes. What they didn't know was hurting them. But we didn't know how to make it better.

I felt responsible for my sons' sorrow. I did not know how to tell Oliver and Evan the story they needed. They needed a *good* story, not the half-baked, vague first draft they'd been distributed in the home workshop. They needed a mournful, unflinching, but also funny, hopeful story, a story of reckoning and acceptance and forgiveness. But I couldn't tell them that story yet, because I was the one who needed to do the reckoning and accepting and forgiving, and I wasn't there yet. Not even close.

What really happened, Daddy? Why are you acting this way? Tell us more about Granny and Grandpa.

EVAN SAID, "YOU can't really say a promise lasts forever. People break promises. A promise is a promise but that doesn't mean it lasts. Sometimes you have a friend and you think they'll be your friend forever but then the next day they don't even act like your friend anymore. That's happened to me."

OLIVER AND EVAN asked about what happened to Granny and Grandpa, all the time. They wanted to know *why*. They asked. They kept asking. Wasn't it my duty, now, to tell?

I know. It's hard.

No, Dad. Why?

Is it permanent?

Will they ever change their minds?

They asked Granny when she came to visit.

They asked Grandpa on the phone.

No one told them *why*.

E.M. Forster, in *Aspects of the Novel*, says that "The king died, and then the queen died," is not a plot.

> "The king died, and then the queen died of grief," is a plot. The time sequence is preserved, but the sense of causality overshadows it. Or again: "The queen died, no one knew why, until it was discovered that it was through grief at the death of the king." This is a plot with a mystery in it, a form capable of high development. It suspends the time sequence, it moves as far away from the story as its limitations will allow.

"The king died, and then the queen died" offers nothing to assuage the powerful human craving to know why. "The king died, and then the queen died" helps no one.

"The king did not die, but he tried to die, and the queen knew why, but she did not die, either, though she felt as if she would die of grief." That's a plot.

"Oliver and Evan and Mommy and Daddy had a fun visit to Granny's and Grandpa's house, and Granny and Grandpa got divorced forever," is not a plot.

A good answer makes the question go away. After a good answer, the question no longer needs to be asked. A good answer is like a good ending to a well-made story. A state of chaos has been brought to rest. One reason we need stories so much is because this satisfying state of affairs happens so infrequently in real life.

Deliberate Withholding

OLIVER KNEW THE LOUIS ARMSTRONG VERSION OF "LET'S Do It (Let's Fall in Love)," so he knew that educated fleas do it. He was savvy and probably knew more at seven-years-old than Christine and I thought he did, but we were pretty sure he didn't know the anatomical particulars of what went where. The sex-talk-with-your-child book that Christine had bought, *WHERE DID I COME FROM? The Facts of Life Without Any Nonsense and With Illustrations*, was still up in our bedroom closet beneath a pile of Christine's fuzzy sweaters.

> We wrote it because we thought you'd like to know exactly where you came from, and how it all happened.
> And we know (because we have children of our own) how difficult it is to tell the truth without getting red in the face and mumbling.

Oliver, and Evan also, knew that some men loved men, and some women loved women, and there was a big debate in the country about gay marriage, and that this was as important to Mommy and Daddy as other issues we cared about, like the war in Iraq. Oliver and Evan knew that their aunt Molly couldn't marry Anne, who was great at Legos and sledding and knew all about Star Wars, and that Molly and Anne had a domestic partnership, which wasn't the same as marriage, and that this wasn't fair. The boys even understood that some people weren't sure whether they were a boy or a girl; they felt somewhere in between, and that this didn't make them strange, because it was completely normal, completely good, completely human – it was the way things were.

In other words, we were doing what we thought God (who was not a he or a she) would want us to do as parents, if God, in fact, even existed. We were raising our children to be liberals with a flair for nuance, erring on the side of complexifying confusion rather than evil, fundamentalist oversimplification.

Should we tell them that Grandpa was gay? Maybe we could tell them that Grandpa was gay for a very long time but he didn't know how to tell Granny the truth. Maybe that was what we should do. Start there. We'd told Oliver and Evan that for so long in America people who were gay were not just treated cruelly but sometimes even murdered, and that this sometimes even happened now. Yes. For a long time people even thought that if you were gay or lesbian that you were crazy. Some people still believed this. Some people even believed that God thought it was a sin to be gay. Hard to believe, but true.

BUT THERE WAS no way we were going to tell the boys anything about suicide. And no way we would tell them something terrible had happened to Grandpa a long time ago, when he was a little boy. Someone had touched his private parts in an awful way that had hurt him very much. No. This someone was his own father. No.

The boys understood that no one was to ever touch their private parts. Oliver was the only one who touched Oliver's private parts. Evan was the only one who touched Evan's private parts. If Oliver or Evan wanted to touch their own private parts, that was just fine, but they should do this privately, like in their own bed, and not out in the open on the living room floor where they were also playing with Legos. Christine had an amazing ability to say exactly this to the boys, especially when they were four and five, in the most kind, offhand way. "Hey, *name of Cooney-Martin boy*, sweetheart, it's just fine if you want to touch your penis, but you should touch your penis in your bunkbed and not out in the living room. You can come back and play with your Legos when you're done." Sometimes *name of Cooney-Martin boy* simply stopped touching his penis and turned more of his attention to his Legos with a kind of casual "Sure, Mom," unspoken recognition. Sometimes *name of Cooney-Martin boy* would stop playing Legos and take his mom up on her suggestion and go to his bunkbed for a while and then come back. At such times, I felt toward Christine the way young, untrained Luke Skywalker feels toward Yoda when he levitates Luke's drowned x-wing fighter out of the Dagobah swamp. *How did you do that?* I watched Christine employ this Jedi suggestion more than a few times before I felt confident enough to attempt it myself. Then I did, and it worked. May the force be with you.

In that first week after my father attempted suicide, Christine asked the boys if Grandpa had ever touched them inappropriately, and they'd said no and gone back to playing with their matchbox cars. I was still in Spokane when this happened, but I knew what their answer would be. My father had never been in any way sexually inappropriate with me. I told Christine this, but I knew she needed to ask anyway. I wanted her to ask. I'd asked my father the same thing.

The day after he came out of his coma, I arrived at the hospital early in the morning, took the elevator up to the fifth floor, to the psychiatric I C U. I sat beside my father. He was not asleep. He was staring blankly at the wall. My mother had already been there, but had gone somewhere, and he was alone in the room. I said, "I need to ask you something."

He looked at me.

"Did you ever, in any way, abuse Oliver or Evan?"

My father did not seem surprised that I asked him this question. He stared at me coldly.

I said, "Some people who are abused end up abusing others. That's how it happens."

My father stared at me some more. Finally he said, "Your mother asked me the same thing. She asked if I ever abused you or your brother. Then she asked if I ever abused your boys." An awful look came into his face, a rageful look I didn't think he was capable of. "I would never hurt a child. I have never abused anyone. Never."

I nodded my head. "I know," I said. "I just needed to hear you say so."

THOSE FIRST MONTHS after my father's suicide, Christine and I talked about what we should tell the boys. I kept bringing it up. I could not help myself. I asked her at night before we went to sleep and in the morning before the kids woke up. I said, "Don't you think we should tell them?" I asked her when we were driving the kids to the swimming pool or to the zoo, so that Oliver or Evan would shout out, "Tell them what? What should you tell us?" Sometimes I said, "When do you think we should tell them?" Because that was a question about timing, and not about whether we would tell them or not. I drank my second cup of coffee and waited for Christine to wake up, and I said, "I think we should tell them today."

Christine didn't think we needed to tell them anything. Not now. They were too little. We would wait until they were older, until they were old enough to understand. And even then, we wouldn't tell them everything. We would tell them that Grandpa was gay, but we might never tell them about incest or suicide. For her, there was no real dilemma.

Besides bringing it up too much, I didn't really argue, but I couldn't come close to Christine's certainty, her conviction. In those first months after my father's suicide attempt, my mind didn't work well. It was all a sad, confusing, inarticulate muddle. In my memory, our conversations ended in paralysis and indecision. But Christine remembers differently. She remembers a fierce clarity, an instinctive determination to protect the boys from psychological harm. She remembers not indecision, but anger at the very fact that our little boys were in danger of ever discovering this knowledge, this truth.

I nodded, I agreed, I said okay. But telling the boys nothing did not sit well with me. The idea that there were things about our family we might never tell the boys burned inside me. And I didn't know why. No, it's more true to say that I didn't think to ask myself why. I just wanted to tell them. I didn't want there to be any secrets between us. I wanted to just start telling them, and see where that lead us. I wanted to tell them more than I wanted to protect them from what I might tell them. I wanted to tell them more than I wanted them to understand. Understanding would come later. A part of me knew this was irrational, though I never articulated it to myself, much less to Christine. So after a while, I stuffed this impulse when it came to me, which was often, sometimes several times a day.

Rocky

I WOKE UP EACH MORNING AT FOUR-THIRTY OR FIVE. I couldn't sleep. I peed. I let Rocky out to pee. I made coffee. I let Rocky back in. I fed him. I was exhausted. I didn't turn the lights on. I sat down at the kitchen table and looked out the window. Mostly I saw my own reflection. My sadness was like a low-grade fever that wouldn't come down. I did not want to "sit" with my feelings, but there I was. I liked to think of myself as "a man of action." Christine sometimes called me "Mr. Incredible" after the chubby, forced-into-early-retirement dad/superhero of the Pixar movie, *The Incredibles*. But there was no villain to defeat, no one to rescue. I could not keep my father from sitting alone at his card table in his cheap apartment. I could not keep him from his shame. I could not keep my mother from reconfiguring her memories, from replaying the tape of thirty-nine years of marriage and doubting even the smallest of moments. I could not return her trust to her. I could not explain to my children why their grandparents had divorced and why I was so sad. There was nothing to do. So I sat there and waited for the day to start. Dawn came slowly. Coffee helped some. Rocky sat at my feet at the kitchen table.

Rocky and I had been spending a lot more time together lately. He had uncanny emotional radar. If someone was sad or having a hard time, Rocky jumped up on the couch beside them, put his head in their lap, and gave them the opportunity to feel better by petting him. If Christine and I had any kind of disagreement, however mild, the winner was the one Rocky stood

beside. It did not matter if you were right. It mattered how sad you were. I did not win often. But that was changing. Rocky liked me better broken. He didn't need to know why. He'd always treated me with the wary affection of the beta male, ever ready to roll over and bare his throat and belly. Now he rested his chin on my slippers, so that I couldn't move my feet. I felt powerfully sorry for myself. I had been cured of my optimism bias and become more like a citizen of Denmark. The Danes, according to *The New York Times*, "are perennial pessimists, always reporting low expectations for the year to come. They then find themselves pleasantly surprised when things turn out rather better than expected."

Subject: **What's going on in my life**

Date Fri, 20 July 2007

I really am sorry I was so inconsiderate for not responding to your email, the book and the CD. I am really appreciative of the Kingston Trio CD. I have it in my CD player in the car (as I don't have one in the apartment) and listen to it anytime I go anywhere. Those are two great albums and bring back many fond memories of my early days as a Folk aficionado. I find myself singing/humming one or another of the tunes frequently at work. I'm glad Oliver is enjoying the water squirter. I picked one with two squirt guns so he could share with Evan and have someone to play with, especially when no other kids were around.

As to what else is going on in my life, it is basically the same as it was before, with the exception that I am unable to share it with Dee, and to share in her daily life. Of course I miss her enormously and will probably do so for the rest of my life. Your Mother was my life. I didn't have friends outside her circle of friends and acquaintances. There is now a gargantuan hole where a normal existence used to be. Don't tell me this isn't penance or consequence. When anyone asks, "How are you?" the response is, "Well, OK" or "As well as can be expected, I guess." I can't even begin to describe the depth of that hole. Now, given that, please don't think that your Mother's grief is not wider and deeper. I am aware that all these years, I knew what I was doing and she didn't. I am also aware of how deeply she loved me and how utterly devastated she must be. As bad as I feel, her pain is worse than mine. I wish there was something I could do to alleviate that pain. I will try to find some way if I can.

Thanks for bringing me to task. I clearly needed it. I love you and please give my love to Christine, Oliver, and Evan – even Rocky.

Dad

Stand and Deliver

THE POET WILLIAM STAFFORD WROTE OF THE "REMOTE important region in all who talk." In 1945, when my father was four years old, that remote, important region inside him was desecrated.

Evan was four years old the summer after my father attempted suicide, and he was an accomplished talker. He talked about past and future playdates, the plots of his favorite cartoons, the girls he and Oliver chased on the playground at the park. He was capable of monologues of ten minutes or more. But there were many moments when I couldn't listen because images of Evan combined with what I imagined had happened to my father into an awful mixture of revulsion and rage and helplessness, and Evan would see that I was not really there, and he'd say, "Daddy, what's the matter?"

ON THE FIRST day of preschool, Evan marched into the bathroom like a kid with something to prove. A few weeks earlier, he'd decided it was time to stand and pee. His aim was unreliable, but that wasn't the point. He was a big boy. He was thirty-seven inches tall, his belly convexly toddlerish, not flat like his seven-year-old brother. He weighed thirty-five pounds. He could pull up his underpants and then his shorts, all by himself, to his great pride and mine. Related complex tasks, once beyond him, had become routine. Standing on the stool in front of the sink, he could:

1. turn on the faucet and wet his hands
2. push down a fat dollop of soap from the dispenser
3. vigorously rub his hands together
4. rinse
5. turn off the faucet, and
6. dry his hands with a towel instead of his shirt.

The preschool bathroom has no door. What is beautiful about this is that Evan and his pre-schoolmates don't care. What is beautiful is their innocence, their trust, their absence of self-consciousness, their absence of shame. They do not need a door. What is abhorrent and ugly is that, because of the corrosion of some people's hearts, there must be no door.

Evan does not need to be protected from me. I did not need to be protected from my father. On the first day of preschool, at the end of the summer of 2007, as Evan was standing and peeing and flushing, as he was washing and drying his hands, I stood in the doorframe and all I wanted to do was scream.

IN *SONG OF MYSELF*, Walt Whitman wrote:

> Unscrew the locks from the doors!
> Unscrew the doors themselves from their jambs!
>
> Whoever degrades another degrades me;
> And whatever is done or said returns at last to me.

The Family Plot

ONE SUNDAY MORNING, I FOUND MYSELF WANDERING through a graveyard near our house, up and down the rows of faded pink cloth roses and sunken headstones. I didn't know a soul buried there, and I didn't know what connection or solace I expected to find. All I knew was that, here, if anywhere, was an object lesson on impermanence: hundreds of graves bordered by a six-lane thruway, a storage warehouse, and two used-car lots packed with balloons and SUVs. There was no entrance, just an opening where the drooping chain-link fence fell apart completely. It looked like an urban vacant lot littered with plastic bags, Styrofoam cups, rusted pipes, and crosses.

For five years, I'd been driving past at forty miles an hour on the way to the boys' preschool, first with Oliver and then with Evan. The graveyard nagged at my conscience. I didn't know why no one picked the place up. I didn't know if this bothered anyone but me. This was the closest cemetery to my home in a quiet neighborhood, less than a mile from the university where I was a teacher, but I didn't know its name.

The first grave beyond the opening in the chain-link fence was the most recent. There was no headstone. A body-sized, dirt mound rose a foot above the earth, surrounded by fist-sized rocks, like a pioneer's grave on the wagon train west, or a potter's field grave, dug quickly and late at night. On a small, green metal stand, in a frame under glass, these words were printed on weathered paper:

There was an address and a phone number for the funeral director. I dialed the number on my cellphone. It rang twice and a man named Ed Hatton answered. He seemed unsurprised by my call and the fact that I was standing at Esteban Salido's grave. He was having Sunday brunch at a restaurant with his family, but he had a few minutes. He seemed like a man accustomed to phone calls involving death and odd circumstances.

He remembered Esteban Salido. I asked him if he knew the
name of the graveyard I was standing in. He didn't. But he said
there were other graveyards like it, family graveyards, spread out
over the Rio Grande Valley. He named one just off the interstate
by the airport and another near the Balloon Fiesta Park. He
interrupted himself to order the ranch omelet and then told me
about the Albuquerque Indian School graveyard, where Pueblo
and Navajo children were buried between 1882 and 1933. There
were no signs now at all of their graves; it was a 4-H park and a
playground. He said I wouldn't believe how many graves get dug
up each year by construction workers. Our connection went
bad for a few seconds but then he was saying how sad it made
him that people were losing the sacred places of their family's
past. I could hear, in the background, the clinking of plates and
forks, but Ed Hatton was unhurried, eloquent, and I stood there
in front of Esteban Salido's grave, under a hot August sun, and
listened. Ed ran a mortuary now, but he had once managed a
number of family cemeteries. So many people now lived far away
from where their loved ones were buried. They had nowhere to
go to mourn. "You have called about something very close to my
heart," he said. I thanked him for taking time away from his family and his breakfast, and he said, "No, thank *you*."

I LEFT BEHIND Estaban Salido's grave and walked among the
haphazard rows of graves, headstones weathered, cracked, the
letters faded or nearly illegible. Some were ringed by rocks, railroad ties, rotted two-by-fours, or bricks. Wooden crosses, rebar
crosses. Discarded pipes and plumbing, a rain-soaked mattress,
faded pink flip-flops, a sun-bleached teddy bear.

All that summer I'd felt out of place in the most literal
sense. Not one of the familiar places in my life – my home, my
neighborhood, my office, the playground, the swimming pool –
gave me any solace. Not one of those places could contain my
sorrow for my father and mother or my own feelings of confusion.
But as I walked among the abandoned dead that August

morning, my heart felt strangely light. I was happier than I had been in months. I was so surprised by the dissonance between the neglect before me and the way I was feeling that I laughed out loud.

A graveyard is a wilderness, a place beyond boundaries, a home for unknowns and loss.

MY FATHER DID not attend his father's funeral. I don't know the name or location of the graveyard where my father's father is buried. I don't know the year he died or how old he was or what condition or event killed him. I never met him. I have never seen his picture. I don't know if my father resembles him, or if I resemble him, or if my sons resemble him. My father rarely spoke of him, except to say that he was a violent drunk who beat his mom and sisters – he never once beat my father.

I don't want to know where my father's father is buried. I don't want to go there with my shovel and my rage and unearth his skeleton and tear it apart, bone by bone, then smash each bone to pieces and take what remains far away to a place where no one ever knew or loved him and scatter it all in a vacant lot.

ON AUGUST 16TH, the same day Christine and I celebrated our tenth wedding anniversary, my parents signed the papers making official their divorce. The next day, my mother's Last Will and Testament arrived in the mail.

> I, DOLORES (DEE) TREMEWAN MARTIN, a single woman, of Spokane, Washington, being of sound and disposing mind and memory, and not acting under any duress, menace, fraud or the undue influence of any persons, make my Last Will and Testament, revoking all previous wills and codicils.

On page three, my mother states that her remains shall be cremated and her ashes buried in Elko, Nevada, in the center of the Tremewan Family Plot.

> My headstone will read: Dolores Tremewan Martin, June 11, 1940–"date of death".

My mother will be buried in the town where she was born, beside her mother and father and sisters, beside her aunts and uncles and cousins, beside the friends of her childhood, and the childhood friends of her parents. My mother has not lived in Elko for more than fifty years.

In the six-page document, there is not a single mention of my father.

My father will be cremated. He has told me that he does not care what happens to his ashes.

MY FATHER'S SUICIDE attempt was an exhumation. The person he could not speak of had been unearthed. My father was more alive, and more alone, than ever.

Epiphany

MY FATHER'S SECRET LIFE WAS UNDONE BY TECHNO-
logical, not social, progress – an innovation known as "tabbed
browsing." He'd recently downloaded the new Microsoft
Internet Explorer 7 on the home computer and was just getting
the hang of it. The window he left open was unincriminating, a
news website; the tabbed window behind this was not. The
pornographic images of men my mother discovered on the
screen left nothing to the imagination.

My father put it this way in an email:

> A small change in the web page structure caught me in an
> unguarded moment and changed the lives of the entire family.

The word "epiphany" comes from an ancient Greek word
meaning "manifestation" or "striking appearance." James Joyce
took this concept and adapted it to his theory of storytelling. In
a letter to his brother Stanislaus, Joyce explained that epiphanies
were "inadvertent revelations ... by which people betrayed the
very things they were most careful to conceal."

The Feast of the Epiphany, in the Catholic liturgical calen-
dar, falls on the 6th of January, but my mother entered the upstairs office and was confronted with an inadvertent revelation
that led to an epiphany on March 17th, St. Patrick's Day. It can't
help that her memories of the men on that computer screen have
become associated with leprechauns.

Much later, my mother told me, "We went to a wedding

that night. Neither one of us said a word. When we came home, I said, 'What is going on?' I hadn't put it together. I can see now that I was in complete denial. We hadn't had sex in more than ten years. When I tried to talk about this with him, he would get angry, come up with all kinds of excuses – like that his back hurt." My mother interrupted herself to laugh out loud. "He refused to see a marriage counselor. He stayed up for hours after I had gone to bed. But I just couldn't see the big picture. I thought it shouldn't matter. We were happy. I didn't want to see the big picture.

"Your father said, 'Do you want me to leave?' I told him I wanted him to tell me the truth. I shouted this at him. I was mad as hell. I still didn't get it. I was thinking, he better give me some explanation. I still thought there must be some explanation, and that this explanation would make things right. That's when he told me that his father had molested him when he was a boy. That he'd been molested for years. But he didn't cry when he told me this. I didn't cry, either. I was too confused, too much in shock."

My mother and father remained living together in a cold, awful silence for six more weeks. My father denied that he was gay. He met her questions with silence. He stared at her until she walked away. Or he walked away. In the mornings, they went to work. In the evenings, they came home, ate dinner and slept in the same bed. They had increasingly escalated arguments. My mother went to see a counselor, who said, "I think your husband is gay." The counselor told my mother to confront him. Ask him. My mother said she already had. The counselor told her to confront him again.

My mother confronted my father again, "Are you gay?"

"No," he said.

My father refused to see this counselor with my mother. My mother told him to pack his bags. My father agreed to see this counselor with my mother.

The counselor asked my father, "Are you gay?"

My father said, "Yes, and I have been all my life."

THESE LONG, AWFUL, six weeks included the non-celebration of their 39th anniversary, on April 1st, which every year is April Fool's Day – a day that had always involved happiness, gratitude, and some kind of playful practical joke, a day that had never before been laced with such poisonous irony. At least not for my mother.

Can We Make Patients Better Off by Prolonging Their Pain?[1]

FOR BOTH MY MOTHER AND FATHER, THE MEMORY OF those six weeks, that time when the life they shared together unraveled, was made measurably worse by my father's suicide attempt, according to the research of the psychologist and Nobel Laureate, Daniel Kahneman.

Kahneman discovered, among other things, that the character of our memory is determined largely by the peak intensity experienced during an episode, and by the intensity of when the episode ends. He found, as you would guess, that less painful endings generated better memories than severely painful endings.[2] But Kahneman also found something deeply counter-intuitive:

> ...an episode of 60 seconds during which one hand is immersed in painfully cold water will leave a more aversive memory than a longer episode, in which the same 60 seconds are followed by another 30 seconds during which the temperature rises slightly. Although the extra 30 seconds are painful, they provide an improved end. When experimental participants are exposed to the two episodes, then given a choice of which to repeat, most choose the longer one.

It follows that if my mother and father had decided to go on a brief golf vacation, as they'd often done in the past, *after* my father's suicide attempt and recovery, then their memories of

---

1   Daniel Kahneman, "Toward a Science of Well-Being" (lecture, Cambridge University, Cambridge, UK, January 27, 2005).

2   Kahneman has said, "You don't need a lot of research to know that sex is better than commuting."

those *six and a half* weeks would be more positive. The golf vacation would have no doubt been difficult, but they both liked to golf, and they could have even booked separate hotel rooms and taken only a few meals together, eating in silence or not, whatever. Most important would be their time together on the tees, fairways, and greens, my mother biting her tongue, struggling to refrain from offering small, constructive pieces of advice on my father's swing. This golfing vacation would not have been nearly so painful as those moments when the fire trucks and ambulances arrived, lights flashing, sirens blaring throughout the Manito Park neighborhood – though my father's memories of these particular moments are hazy. He was still conscious at that point but fading fast. Soon afterward, there is a two-day period of which he has no aversive memories at all, because he was in a coma.

According to Kahneman, rememberers suffer "duration neglect":

> By collapsing experience into moments, they seem to lose almost all impact of duration ... The overall impression is determined as an average of how people felt at the peak and at the end.

My mother is a Public Choice economist. Almost forty years ago, she wrote her dissertation under the direction of James Buchanan, who, like Kahneman, is a Nobel Laureate in Economics, though Jim, as my mother calls him, wasn't a laureate back then, not yet. So, for a long time, my mother has been a scholar interested in rational choices. But even had she known about the upside, memory-wise, of one more golf vacation together, I doubt my mother would have chosen this option. She does not want better memories. She does not want any memories.

My father would have chosen the golf vacation. He knows all too well that bad memories are to be feared.

Cold Case

MY BAD MEMORIES FROM CHILDHOOD WERE NOTHING like my father's. Still, after my father's suicide attempt, certain bad memories from my childhood kept coming back to me, nagging at me, daring me to puzzle them out.

When I was thirteen, my mother was granted a sabbatical from the University of Nebraska, where she was an economics professor, and our family left Lincoln and moved to Rockville, Maryland. My mother took a position as a fellow in an economic think-tank in D.C. This was my freshman year in high school. My sophomore year, we returned to Lincoln, ostensibly because my mother needed to return to teaching at the university. But my mother had worked out an understanding with her department – and with my father – and she took a job as an economic analyst in the Reagan White House. I was not party to these negotiations. My mother remained in D.C., flying back to visit us in Lincoln one weekend each month.

I missed my mother terribly. She'd always been the one I confided in, looked to for guidance or encouragement, the one I wanted to talk to most, about anything, the one whose recognition I coveted and worked hard to earn. How do you explain why someone makes you laugh, or feel at ease, or valued, important, distinct, cherished? How do you explain that the simple presence of a person makes the world feel less cold?

I did not understand why my mother had chosen to live away from us. Why did our family have to be separated? If my mother's career opportunities were too good to pass up, great, but why couldn't we have *all* just stayed in D.C.? So what if we needed to get the house in shape to sell? We didn't need to live in it for that to happen. These were lousy reasons to split up a family. It didn't make sense. It seemed like her choice only, an abandonment I couldn't explain to myself, no matter how many times I turned it over in my mind. It never occurred to me that she might have been pushed. It never occurred to me that my father, like Iago whispering in Othello's ear, only appeared to have my mother's best interests, and all of our best interests, in mind.

When my mother flew back from D.C. that winter for Christmas, she was not herself. She had always been intense, passionate, willful. But now she spoke too quickly. She stood in our living room, her eyes too wide, waving her arms wildly. She told us, breathlessly, that there had been a miracle. Her flight had passed through a storm somewhere over the Midwest–through terrible turbulence. The plane was going down and should have crashed. Everyone should have died. But God had saved them.

I had never seen my mother behave this way before– fast talking and arm waving. She wasn't overly religious. The miracle of the loaves and the fishes, in our house, was a parable, a biblical tall tale. We all knew the difference between literal truth and underlying mystery. But on this night, my mother claimed that God had spoken to her directly. God had told her that she should not fear. For her flight would pass through the storm and be brought down to rest in safety.

I did not believe her. She was not to be believed. I don't remember looking to my father for some explanation. I try to remember what happened next, how the remainder of my mother's first evening home played out, but there's nothing there.

Then my mother was in bed and could not speak. I remember a period of several weeks when she lay in bed, catatonic. I remember her nightgown unbuttoned too far and her thin, veined hand absently scratching at an exposed nipple. She was completely unable to respond, unable to even acknowledge me, though her eyes were open. There was no way to break her silence. I yelled at her. I yelled that she was not my mother. But she could not respond. The most she could do was turn her head and look to the wall instead of the ceiling.

My mother says now, "I remember you yelling at me, that I was not your mother. But I couldn't answer."

I remember, later, running after her through the snow. It was a cold, overcast afternoon. She'd gotten past us, out the front door somehow, and was making her way down the block toward my old elementary school. She was in her slippers and nightgown, carrying her briefcase, which was empty. She'd recently regained the power to speak, and she told me she was late for work. She could not keep them waiting. She had to hurry. I took her by the elbow and steered her back home. I helped her back inside, upstairs, sat her on the bed, and I took her soaked slippers off her feet and helped her back under the covers.

I remember red, cold, bony feet and opening her briefcase to find it empty. But most of my memories of this time have the quality of a bad lyric poem – full of the kind of atmospheric imprecision I have no patience for. I want to know what happened. Why not just say what happened? But I can't. I can't remember.

I remember sitting in the front row of Cathedral of the Risen Christ Church. My mother had insisted we go to 10:30 a.m. mass, insisted we all sit in our usual place in the front pew. Off and on throughout the service, my mother wept. She wailed. Caterwauled. There was no other sound. I tried to get her to leave the pew, no genuflecting, just leave, just walk down the aisle and outside. The priest continued saying the mass, as if nothing out of the ordinary was happening, displaying a Catholic willingness to ignore calamity that should surprise no one.

My mother would not be moved. Her wailing still rings in my ears.

My father told me that the muscles in my mother's neck were too tense; the muscles were constricting the flow of blood to her brain. She just needed to rest. The muscles in her neck would eventually relax, and she'd be herself again. She did not need to go to the hospital. He did not utter words like "psychiatrist," "manic-depression," "bipolar." He would not even say, "nervous breakdown," though I heard other people say this, in my presence, about my mother. He did not tell me about the time my mother escaped from a mental hospital when I was ten. He did not tell me she'd once admitted herself to a mental hospital before I was born. My father did not even say the word "crazy."

I wanted to know why. Why couldn't my mother even speak to me? Would she ever get better? Did she know what was happening to her? How much did she understand? Would this awful feeling in my heart ever go away? I don't know that I ever asked my father any of these questions directly. I don't think so. I can't remember. But I will never forget the power of those unacknowledged feelings – confusion and helplessness, fear and grief.

It occurs to me now that here is one reason why it was so completely unacceptable that my sons did not know why their grandparents had divorced. They were confused and sad, and I had an explanation, and I was keeping it from them, and this unspoken explanation was intimately related to other unspoken explanations – a chain of secrets and unacknowledged sadness that now ran through me to them.

LATE ONE NIGHT, that winter I was fifteen, I "stole" our red Ford Escort wagon. I only had my learner's permit and so wasn't legal to drive on my own. Sometime after midnight, I silently rolled the car out of the driveway, turned the key in the ignition halfway down the block, and drove to my girlfriend's house. Or at least I thought of her as my girlfriend; she had a boyfriend off at college who was shorter than me. My father was awake and discovered first the car, then me, missing. I'm speculating, but perhaps he missed the car because he was planning to go somewhere himself. Perhaps he was planning to meet someone, someone anonymous. One more person who didn't know him.

About an hour after I arrived at my girlfriend's house, my brother showed up. He said, "You should go home." When I came in the kitchen door around two in the morning, my father was sitting at the table. My mother was upstairs, in bed, but it's not quite right to say that she was asleep. She mumbled at all hours. Sometimes her eyes were open, sometimes not. My father did not yell at me. Nor did he commiserate, regaling me with his own late night escapades, hamstrung by desire. In a leap of logic that only now makes sense, my father told me that he wanted me to talk to Monsignor Crowley. I didn't have to make a confession. I just had to talk. So, that very next day, Monsignor Crowley and I talked, though I don't remember the conversation or even where it took place.

If you could have seen me during this time, walking the halls of my high school, attending class, at basketball practice with my teammates, there would have been no way for you to surmise that all was not well at home. I was engaged, purposeful, kind. I kept earning straight As. I raised my hand in class, though not too much, and either I knew the answer or was willing to speculate. I never said it aloud to anyone, much less silently to myself, but I was troubled.

My mother's madness diminished like an echo. She returned to herself. She did not talk about what had happened to her any more than my father talked about what had happened to her. Or what had happened to him. I did not want to bring up what had happened out of the fear that at the mention of certain words or phrases or events she might start wailing again. I did not know how fragile she was – or I was – and so I assumed the worst and buried my need for explanation.

At the end of that year, my mother left her job at the university, we sold the house on Stratford Avenue, and we moved back to the D.C. area, where we bought a house in Falls Church, Virginia. To say that I didn't like attending three different high schools in three years in three different states is an understatement I wasn't capable of then.

During that time, I perfected a skill I'd been learning all my life, a skill that had been modeled for me since the day I was born, a skill that I have to this day in all kinds of contexts and situations – the ability to maintain a veneer of equanimity, a surface polish, a detachment from my emotional life, that I no longer trust. Because, then and now, it is not an act, not a conscious one anyway. I have even myself fooled.

TWENTY YEARS LATER, after a mysterious suicide attempt, like a cold case detective presented with crucial new clues, I started piecing a few things together. I understood that my father might not have minded those months of separation. Not so much. That time he spent parenting us alone while my mother remained in D.C. – maybe that wasn't so bad for him. I had always assumed it to be a tremendous hardship for him. It certainly was for me.

One summer night, I interrogated my father on this issue. What really happened is that I started shouting.

"Didn't you *want* that to happen? Didn't you *engineer* that to happen? Didn't you want her to be halfway across the country? Didn't you play the part of the martyr? Wasn't that an act? Didn't you love that you could come and go late at night without any chance of being caught out? Didn't you feel responsible for pushing her away? Do you think that had *anything* to do with her losing her mind? Do you think that would have happened if we'd all been together?"

My father tried to respond, but I cut him off.

"Why won't you just admit it? She was *in your way*. She was *always* in your way. Wasn't it nice to finally get her out of the way?"

I had not shouted at my father once since his suicide attempt. I had not shouted at him since I was a teenager. But now I shouted these questions and accusations into the phone, delivering each with cold, relentless force, like clubhunting a seal on the ice.

My father yelled back at me once or twice, but halfheartedly, and eventually I wore him down. He couldn't match my resolve. Finally, resigned, defeated, he said, "Yes. I knew what I was doing. I wanted it to happen. I looked forward to the time your mother would be gone."

"I knew it," I said, and hung up on him.

The Best Medicine

I STRUGGLED WITH MY SENSE OF HUMOR.

Just weeks after my father attempted suicide, in a daring stakeout and crackdown on depravity, Idaho Senator Larry Craig was arrested by a plainclothes policeman for lewd toe-tapping in a Minneapolis airport restroom stall. Craig's righteous, indignant, "wide-stance" denial deserved to be ridiculed. When the story broke, responsible comedy outlets took up the cause. But I could not laugh about hardcore conservative, rabidly anti-gay, straight-identified but who-did-he-think-he-was-kidding Larry Craig. I just ... couldn't. I intellectually understood that acid mockery was a powerful weapon in the battle against the evil forces of bigotry, and that the more innocent, unsuspecting citizens who could be brought, however reluctantly, to laugh at homophobia, the more homophobics would be vanquished. I knew that the purpose of satire, as Mark Twain put it, was, "the deriding of shams, the exposure of pretentious falsities, and the laughing of stupid superstitions out of existence."

But I could not bridge the gap between wanting to laugh about Larry Craig and laughing about Larry Craig. I could barely manage a sad smirk. David Letterman said,

> Several prominent Republicans are calling on Senator Larry Craig to resign. And a couple are asking for his phone number.

In an interview Larry Craig and his wife gave to *The Today Show*'s Matt Lauer, Suzanne Craig said,

> I knew immediately it was not the truth because the description
> he gave of Larry in some areas that only I might know about were
> wrong, on three counts.

Jon Stewart said,

> Count number one: his balls are not plum-sized. They are, at best,
> apricot-like. Secondly, the description of his penis as "inside
> another man," that has not been my experience...

My father? Gay? My sixty-six year old father? That had not
been my experience. How had I missed that? Hadn't I been
paying attention? But when my father first told me he was gay,
that afternoon in the ICU, in his hospital gown, I knew it to be
true, though I had never once suspected it. I felt surprise followed
immediately by inevitability. No. Yes. It was only later, when the
shock of those days began to wear off that I felt impugned. Stupid.
What I couldn't reconcile, and what I struggle to reconcile even
still, was the most common of feelings – *I thought I knew him*. If I
didn't know my own father, who else did I not know?

Inquisition

I PUMMELED MY FATHER WITH QUESTIONS. WHEN DID he first admit to himself that he was gay? Where did he go to have anonymous sex in Nebraska? Where did he go in New Jersey? In Virginia? In New Mexico? Had he ever had a relationship? Had he ever wanted one? Had he ever known socially the men he knew sexually? How could he have been such a political conservative all those years? Was he still a Republican? How much did he worry that he would be caught? Had he known all along that he would attempt suicide if he were caught? When did his father stop abusing him? Why didn't he tell my mother about his father's abuse? Had he worked as a traveling pharmaceutical representative so he could be gone for multiple days in a row and not have to be so cautious about being caught? Was that part of his conscious thinking? Did he tell himself that he couldn't tell my mother the truth because he was afraid that she might have another "breakdown"? Did he tell himself that his care for my mother while she was manic or catatonic somehow made up for his secret life? Did he tell himself that she would not be able to go on without him?

Question after question in no particular order. There was vengeance in these questions, a satisfying vindictiveness. I knew most of these questions, if not all, were excruciating for him. But part of me wanted to hurt him, wanted him to suffer these questions as some small penance for all the pain he had caused.

But behind this, also, was a sincere desire to know him. Who *are* you?

He told me about the rest areas off the interstate near Portales, New Mexico, and Morristown, New Jersey, about the public restroom near Children's Zoo in Lincoln, Nebraska, about the basement bathroom at the community college in Rockville, Maryland. He never invited a man into our home. It always happened in a public place. When I asked him how it could possibly be that he never got AIDS, he didn't say anything for a very long time.

Then he said, "I was always oral."

Now it was my turn to be quiet. I didn't want to know this, but I had wanted an answer, and he'd given me one. Finally, I said, "You can get AIDS that way."

He said, "It's not nearly as likely."

"Didn't you worry that you would give Mom AIDS?"

"Yes, I did. I worried about that."

On the phone, my father answered my questions, one by one, with reluctance and resentment and without elaboration.

No. He'd never had any relationship with any man. He'd never wanted one. He had a relationship with my mother.

Email was different. In writing, he sometimes went on at length, telling me about his past, his feelings, then and now. Perhaps this was better persona management on his part. Perhaps it was easier for him to be the person he thought I wanted him to be – thoughtful, reflective, remorseful – over email. How was I to know whether my father actually meant what he said? After all, he'd spent his entire life successfully being the person other people wanted him to be. But I felt that too much was at stake between us for cynicism. Anger, yes. Cynicism, no. Trust was a choice. When the suspicion that I was being played for forgiveness occurred to me – and it did often – I chased it from my mind.

After a while, I ran out of steam. I didn't know the next question to ask. But I still didn't feel satisfied. I needed my father to do some of the asking now – questions for himself that he didn't already know the answers to, and some questions for me. But I didn't make that clear. Nothing was clear to me then. So we lapsed into silence broken intermittently by conversations about work and new furniture and three-inch-thick science fiction paperbacks.

My father would disappear from my thoughts for days, and I'd wonder why I had such a strange ache in my chest. Oh. Yeah. My father wanted to disappear – from my thoughts, from his own thoughts. He wanted to go away. I wanted to let him go, and didn't want to, at once. A day or two after recognizing this strange ache, I'd call. He'd tell me about how his work was going, how many patients he had on his caseload at the nursing home. He'd tell me about the science fiction novels he was reading – plots, characters, settings. He was flying through them, staying up late reading, reading, reading, sometimes until three or four in the morning. He couldn't remember the last time he'd done that; it had been years and years. Sometimes he asked about the boys or Christine, and I would talk for a while. There was relief in his voice when the conversation ended after ten minutes or so. Just because that part of him that had always been in hiding was now exposed didn't mean he was going to stop trying to hide it. But to hide that part of him, he had to hide all of himself, from me anyway, the one with all the probing questions.

Renunciation

WHEN MY FATHER DESCRIBED HIMSELF READING SCIENCE fiction deep into the night, I understood that he was not just taking a little break from an otherwise fearless and searching personal inventory. Some might deride my father's reading as lowbrow – it was, after all, *genre* fiction. I didn't care about that. I had no problem with science fiction. But my father was not supposed to be absorbed in pleasure. Not when I couldn't sleep for five consecutive hours. He didn't get to escape to another galaxy. He hadn't earned that yet.

Studying philosophy in college, I'd learned a little about the long discourse and debate about the nature of happiness. My father was not pursuing *eudaimonia* – Aristotle's notion of the life well-lived. The virtuous life. A happiness that wasn't really happiness – the emotional experience – but a path to aspire to and follow, a *way* of living, a "human flourishing," rather than a feeling in a particular moment, or in my father's case, hours of moments, until three or four in the morning.

Neither was my father's happiness the brand spoken of by the bald Buddhist photographer monk Matthieu Ricard, who lived in a hermitage in the Himalayas and was buddies with the Dalai Lama. Ricard was once a biochemist and had written extensively about Buddhism and science and happiness. Ricard had volunteered for thousands of hours of neuroscience research on the long-term effects of meditation on the brain, after which it was determined that Ricard was "the happiest man alive."

About this designation, Ricard has said, "It's a joke which I find difficult to get rid of."

Ricard's Buddhist notion of happiness is better described as "well-being," or better yet: "a deep sense of serenity and ful-fillment, a state that pervades and underlies all emotional states, including all the joys and sorrows that can come one's way." It isn't to be confused with pleasure, not even hours of it.

> Pleasure is contingent upon time, upon its object, upon the place. It is something which changes its nature. Beautiful chocolate cake, first serving delicious, second not so much, then we feel disgust…

My father had never experienced Buddhism's deep serenity. Not many people had. I sure hadn't. But that's what I wanted for him, anyway. I wanted him to be all done with pleasure. I wanted a deep searching that would lead him to something true and authentic and lasting. What did he have to lose? I wanted his sui-cide attempt and his permanent estrangement from my mother to take him somewhere. I wanted him to hit the existential road. I wanted him to start healing the deep psychological wounds he'd had since childhood, and I knew he couldn't get there on his own. I didn't want him to become a sexless eunuch, struggling to maintain a one-legged yoga pose in loose-fitting clothes. But I didn't want him to sit in a La-Z-Boy in his cheap apartment all alone reading science fiction, either. I wanted him to stop being one of those "suspicious people in vehicles" at the park.

A couple of weeks before his suicide attempt, on my mother's orders, my father started seeing a counselor. (My mother knew he had been molested as a child, but he hadn't yet admitted to being gay.) After his discharge from the hospital, he kept going to this counselor, or claimed to be going, anyway. But a few months later, sometime that summer, he stopped going. He told me that he didn't think he needed to go anymore. I was speechless. For about a minute. This infuriated me. No. It's more true to say that it hurt me. I wanted a real relationship with my father, and I wanted him to do the work, yes, for his own good, but also I wanted him to do the work for me, for the sake of our relationship. It didn't matter if my father didn't think he was worth the trouble. Wasn't I worth it?

It took a long time for me to realize that I felt this way. When I told Christine my revelation, she said, "You hear that all the time in Al-Anon. 'Why won't they just stop drinking for me?' You know that expression 'Expectations are premeditated resentments.'"

Right. I'd heard that. I just didn't realize it applied to me.

In those first few months after his suicide attempt, I expected a lot from my father, and I expected it ASAP. I was like one of those animal rights activists who sneaks into the zoo, breaks the locks and flings open the cages, and yells at the lemurs and komodo dragons and koala bears, *Let's Go! Let's Go! Let's Go!* But the lemurs just eat their bananas, and the komodo dragons don't even blink or flick their forked tongues, and the koala bears grip their branches more tightly, turning their heads against all the noise. They don't think they need to go to counseling.

When I told Christine about my father's science fiction reading, it didn't make her angry or exasperated. It made her sad. She said, "He's barely hanging on." I tried not to listen. Christine's wisdom did not conform to or reinforce my plan for my father. Not after all he had done.

Ricard says,

No one wakes up in the morning and says, "May I suffer all day."

I did not want my father to suffer all day. But I wanted monastic renunciation. And not the smiling Buddhist kind with snow-swept Himalayan vistas. I wanted medieval Catholic asceticism, the cold and damp kind, with stone floors, hairshirts, bad haircuts. I wanted atonement, not serenity. I wanted him out wandering the eastern Washington high desert, eating locusts, for forty days and forty nights, a number I understood to be the biblical signifier for a really long time.

I wanted my father to be the virtuous man I'd always

thought him to be. I wanted rectitude and dignity. I wanted him to be the man who was an usher every Sunday at 10:30 a.m. mass, the man who drove me on countless early weekday mornings, for four straight years, fifth grade through eighth grade, to church so that I could serve as an altar boy for the 6:30 a.m. mass, for Fathers Morganthou and Vasa and Monsignor Crowley.

Never once, not one morning, in all those years, through all those long Nebraska winters, did I miss my turn in the rotation to serve 6:30 a.m. mass. I was never even late. I would remember. When it was cold – it was often below zero – my father went out ten minutes before we needed to leave, unplugged the heater block, and started up his big, white Chrysler Newport, with its push button transmission down the left hand of the dash and its pale green interior illumination.

My father sat in the pews, in the small side chapel, with the five or six other parishioners, the two or three nuns, while I rang the bells and washed the priest's hands with holy water poured from the small, cut glass carafe, and the priest whispered from Psalm 51: "Lord, wash away my iniquity; cleanse me from my sin."

After we had all recited the Lord's Prayer – the Our Father – the priest said:

> Deliver us, Lord, from every evil, and grant us peace in our day. In your mercy keep us free from sin and protect us from all anxiety as we wait in joyful hope for the coming of our Savior, Jesus Christ.

Before offering communion, the priest said:

> This is the Lamb of God who takes away the sins of the world. Happy are those who are called to his supper.

And my father responded with the others in one voice:

> Lord, I am not worthy to receive you, but only say the word and I shall be healed.

Then I held the copper paten under my father's chin as he knelt at the communion rail and received the body of Christ on his tongue. After mass, I changed out of my black robe and went out to find my father, alone in the chapel and often still on his knees in the pew, his eyes closed in prayer. I'd wait, sitting beside him, until he opened his eyes, smiled and said, "Ready, son." Then, we went out into the first light of morning and drove home.

I think now that he could not wait to be there in that small side chapel. I could not wait to be there with him – I loved those mornings with him – the two of us driving there and back in the quiet of that big car. Or at least I cherish those memories now. Research shows that I have little authority to speak on behalf of the fleeting emotional states of my former self. That was thirty years ago. Even just writing this paragraph damages my ability to act as credible proxy for that brown-haired, black-robed boy. We remember best and most not what we experience, but what we say about what we experience.

Did I admire that man who waited for me in the pew, whose eyes were closed in a seriousness I can only now understand? I don't know. I doubt I gave it much thought.

I could not have known then that my father understood himself to be a sinner – and not just the confess-your-three-sins variety, but the real thing. He believed, fully and sincerely, that he would go to hell for his sins. I could not have known that the church was his place to be quiet and honest with himself, to repent, to beseech God for a forgiveness he could not bring himself to ask of my mother, forgiveness for a sin of betrayal that he knew he would commit again.

Monsignor Crowley knew that my father was gay. He knew that my father had been molested by his own father. Monsignor Crowley was the only person who knew. My father went to Monsignor Crowley once a month for confession. He told Monsignor Crowley everything, and Monsignor Crowley kept his secret. The secret was between my father, Monsignor Crowley, and God.

Until now I'd never stopped to wonder why I wanted to be an altar boy so badly, why for years I served at mass, gladly, unresentfully. It was a duty I performed that did not feel like a duty. It felt like grace. I could not wait to become an altar boy in fifth grade. I had always thought that it was because I was so good at being an altar boy, so devoted and concentrated, that in eighth grade, Monsignor Crowley chose me to be the one altar boy to routinely get out of school and serve at the funeral masses that took place across the parking lot in the church, the one boy who got to drive with him out to the cemetery in the long procession of cars, the two of us in that huge space with the facing seats in the back of the black limousine. It never occurred to that me that he might be concerned about me, because he knew more about my father than I did.

As his special way of showing his concern, Monsignor Crowley would come find me in the robe room maybe ten minutes before mass was to start, and he'd ask me if I wanted to make a confession. Often I would, especially in seventh and eighth grades. I'd follow him into a small side room. We'd sit in chairs opposite each other, our knees almost touching. I was not nervous. Or, I should say that I was not nervous because of anything I feared from him. My fear was more like performance anxiety before an unburdening of pent-up guilt. Sometimes I simply recited my sins. Sometimes Monsignor would ask me directly, his voice soft and gentle, almost a whisper. "Did you have impure thoughts again?"

"Yes, Monsignor."

"Did you act on these thoughts."

"Yes."

"Recite with me the act of contrition."

> Oh my God, I am heartily sorry for having offended thee, and I detest the loss of heaven and the pains of hell, but most of all because I have offended thee, my God, who is all good and deserving of all my love. I firmly resolve, with the help of thy grace, to confess my sins, do penance, and to amend my life, Amen.

"Now, for your penance, say three Our Fathers, and four Hail Marys."

Then it was over. I was left alone in the room to say my

prayers, which I did, penitently. My conscience was now clear, my soul purified, and I could receive communion without sin. Then I went out and served mass. Never once did Monsignor Crowley act sexually inappropriately with me – unless you consider the scene I just sketched to be sexually inappropriate, or, I don't know, creepy.

I AM WEARY of the word "soul." And not just because I no longer believe one exists. For more than a decade, I have suffered the word's overuse by a veritable multitude of undergraduates in their personal essays. I no longer permit them to use the word "soul" in their essays, not for the sixteen weeks they are in my class. It's on the syllabus. I'm no advocate of suppression of speech; it's generally not a good idea, but I had to do something. I explain on the first day that I'm not trying to change or put down their beliefs, but that this policy is simply in their own best grading interests.

But there's no doubt in my mind now that while I was up there on the altar as a boy, lighting candles and ringing the bells, my father was below me, on his knees in the pew, trying to save his soul.

AFTER THE PEDOPHILE scandal broke, my father stopped going to mass. He could not bear to be Catholic. He could not even speak of the church without his voice rising and then breaking in betrayal and abandonment, his face flushed in not just anger, but rage, in who knows how many emotions. I remember being utterly baffled by the emotional intensity of his response. He'd been raised Baptist but converted to Catholicism to marry my mother. He had the convert's zeal for more than thirty years, until molestation after molestation appeared in the newspapers, until church documents showed, over and over, that molestations were kept secret, that records of alleged complaints were deliberately destroyed, and predatory priests were shuffled from parish to parish and never referred to criminal authorities.

Taboo Studies

MY FATHER WENT TO WORK, WATCHED TV, AND READ industrial quantities of science fiction. Time was passing. He was getting through the days. But getting by wasn't good enough. Not for me. Disappointment was always in my silence at the other end of the line when he was speaking.

I sent my father two books via Amazon.com. One was about adult male survivors of incest. The other was about gay men coming out of the closet and trying to find intimacy after years of anonymous sex. I sent him articles from *The New York Times* about people leading secret lives and about the astonishing number of men my father's age, who, in the past decade, were tumbling out of their Fibber McGee closets, and not wearing their Robin Williams *Birdcage* South Beach drag queen costumes, but dressed just in their regular, everyday outfits. The culture was changing fast, and my father was right in the middle of it.

I sent my father pithy, deeply relevant quotes, like this one: "It is a joy to be hidden, but a disaster not to be found." Dr. Donald W. Winnicott said this, whoever he was. I can think, now, of a few who might disagree. Saddam Hussein. Sasquatch. I came across this quote somewhere in my voracious reading on the topic of secret lives. Not much else interested me. What the hell did I know about the relationship between joy and disaster and hiding, other than what I had read in a book?

I do not like myself when I act like I have it all figured out. A know-it-all. Or at least I don't like myself when I recognize this behavior. I often take great satisfaction in mocking my self-satisfaction. But my postmodern meta-smugness abandoned me in those months after my father's suicide. I was sick inside with undifferentiated hurt, and I could not find a way to interact with my father that felt authentic – gentle, accepting, betrayed, angry, demanding, challenging – none of it felt right. My self-help bullying was yet another pose to strike in my confusion.

My father read these books and articles, quotes and emails, dutifully, like a teenager under pressure to get better grades in a taboo curriculum. This dutifulness was in his tone when we spoke. My tone was all too often unmistakable. *How dare you, after all you've done, not read with robust enthusiasm these incredibly particularized self-help books I've sent you?* When he stopped seeing a therapist, my father may not have expected that one of his sons would try to fill this role. Or he may have expected exactly that – I am not hard to figure out and he's known me a long time. So maybe he was "taking his medicine," a cliché with a wider range of meaning for me since his overdose. He probably felt that this was the price he had to pay to have a relationship with me, and he couldn't afford to lose another relationship.

Burn

I HAVE A PICTURE ON MY DESK OF OLIVER AND EVAN standing in Vallecito Lake, in southwestern Colorado. They are walking away from the camera, Oliver leading and Evan following close behind. Evan is in up to his chest. The cold, mountain water is at the top of Oliver's thighs, at the shock-line, and so in this moment, or the moment just before or after, he shivers. Christine took the picture at twilight, the summer after my father attempted suicide. The lake is a darker blue than the light blue sky. All around Oliver and Evan, grass and cattails sprout from the water. In the distance, evergreens angle down the mountains toward shore. More than half of these trees are dead, burnt black

from the Missionary Ridge fire that scorched this wilderness in the summer of 2002. You can almost see this in the picture – the distant trees are not as green as they might be – but there is no mistaking it if you know why.

Subject: **The Book**

Date: Thurs, 9 Aug 2007

Hi Greg,

I hope the week in Colorado was as fun as I suspect it was.

I have been reading the book, but not with the intensity of the weeks before, mainly because I was just tired. If you have gotten up to chapter 6, many of the questions you've been asking will be answered, especially about why I didn't want to share my problem with anyone and why it was important to try with all my available energy to keep it hidden. My feelings resonated throughout chapter 6. The author states quite clearly that many sections of the book will not relate directly to every reader, but I felt this section covered most of my bases. I did hide behind a huge mask of pretense, just to have what I felt would be a normal life. As it turns out, I never had a normal life without pretense and a false front. During all those years, that concept never crossed my mind. Chapter 6 points out very clearly that I was just trying to survive, which is another concept that I never realized. Now, I recognize I am and have been a survivor all these years without ever knowing it consciously. What I did know fairly early on was that I enjoyed being in the company of intelligent people, people who behaved decently and didn't use rough language.

You ask what I am doing for a social life, nothing active. I am going deliberately slowly so as to keep my head screwed on and not jeopardizing my personal feelings and personal safety. I know from other's experience that it would be easy to rebound into an unhealthy relationship. You know what your Mom says, "it is better to not have what you want than to have something you don't want and can't get rid of." That is very sound advice.

You said in your last email that you suspect that I am responding to your emails out of a sense responsibility to you. That is true to some extent, but it is also a way of coercing me into delving deeper into the mystery of who I really am. I remember saying quite forcefully that I am the same person I have always been, the same person you've always known. I think I realize now that is only partially true. The person you've always known is still here, but the inside is different, even to me.

Anyway, Greg, I find it comforting that you feel the need to make claims on me. You have always been a critical judge of the people selected to be part of your life. It would probably require a change of personality to not want to tread lightly and critically around me until you're sure who I really am. Am I the same person you've always known? No. I'm a lot the same, but will hopefully grow more different as I continue to delve into my memories, experiences, and future possibilities of who I will become. There are lots of question marks right now. Thankfully, I'm still alive to look forward to finding the answers.

I have a friend who has offered to introduce me to two male couples to kind of help me find a route or introduction into that community. She will try to set up a small party at her house to meet each other. That I am looking forward to. That could be the start of a social life and would be a welcome change.

Well, I think I've bent your ear long enough. Please give Christine, Oliver, and Evan a hug and a kiss from me. Write again when you can.

Love you,

Dad

The White Bear

PSYCHOLOGISTS ESTIMATE THAT TEN TO FIFTEEN PER-
cent of the population are particularly adept at repressing
unwanted thoughts. "Repressors score low on questionnaires that
measure anxiety and defensiveness," writes Benedict Carey in
The New York Times. "Some psychologists believe they have
learned to block distressing thoughts by distracting themselves
with good memories. Over time – with practice, in effect – this
may become habitual, blunting their access to potentially humili-
ating or threatening memories and secrets."

I tried to imagine my father practicing his good memories
the way I once practiced the piano, the way he once practiced
the guitar. But I didn't know what his good memories were. My
own memories – images and associations and feelings – were
roiling inside me, adapting to what I knew now.

Subject:

Date: Sat, 25 Aug 2007

Hi Greg.

Sorry to be so long in responding to your very interesting email. I read
the New York Times article and find it provocative. There is no doubt that
I did lead a double life for a long time. I'm not sure how much anxiety
and stress I felt at the time due to the distance of time, but I do remember worrying about being discovered. I also remember being very careful and taking great precautions to keep the one life separated from

the other. I never allowed anyone from the other life into my "real" life. I have always been very good at keeping secrets. I remember your Mom was amazed that I could wrap Christmas packages, even my own without looking/peeking to see what it was. On the other hand, I've never tried to be another person than I am. I've never pretended I was somebody other than who I am on the other side. As I've stated several times, I am still the person everyone has always known. The secret person never acted as someone else. I have, however, never given my real name if someone asked. I don't think that is acting or pretending, it's just prudent.

As to repression of thoughts, yes, that is something I have always been able to do. I don't, however, think that is really very unusual in the real world. I'm quite sure that heterosexual people of both sexes are confronted frequently by someone of the opposite sex who exhibits qualities that incite thoughts of "Wow, what a hottie! I'll bet that would be great in bed." Pardon the poor phraseology, but you get what I mean. These thoughts are transient and never acted on but, never the less, do stir the emotions a bit.

As you know, this past week has been very difficult for me. I'm sure that is part of the reason for the delay in responding. I have been depressed by the finality of the divorce. I still wish we could have worked it out differently, but that was not meant to be. I'm not sure I can articulate my feelings just yet, they are still being ruminated deep in my brain, but I am beginning to feel less depressed and more open to moving on with a positive outlook.

Will close for now. I love you. Please give my love to Christine, Oliver, and Evan.

Dad

I DID NOT doubt that my father was a talented repressor. Far more talented than me, that's for sure. For days, I tried, without success, to put out of my mind two particular sentences my father had written in his email from August 25th:

"Wow, what a hottie. I'll bet that would be great in bed."

When I first read these words, I thought, "No. No, Dad, please." But it was no use. The damage had been done. I could not shake these words loose. These phrases – this phraseology – kept coming back to me, at the grocery store, stuck in traffic, riding my bike to work, and even when I was all alone.

 IN A STUDY by the psychologist Daniel Wegner, participants were asked to not think about a white bear, to put any thought of a white bear out of their mind. These participants could not stop thinking about a white bear. Wegner writes, "People who are prompted to try not to think about a white bear while they are thinking out loud will tend to mention it about once a minute."

I called my father and told him about the white bear. He said, "I was always afraid that I was going to somehow mention it, blurt it out. That fear was always somewhere in the back of my mind."

Late at night, when his family was asleep, my father drove to darkened city parks; he drove I-80 to the bathrooms of rest areas. Early the next morning, he often woke beside my mother in a cold sweat, terrified he had spoken in his sleep.

The day after he told me this on the phone, my father wrote in an email, "I can't answer any more of those kinds of questions."

Subject

Date: Sun, 7 Sept 2007

Hi Greg,

Haven't heard from you lately, so I thought I bring you up to date on recent happenings. I am buying a condo. It is in Spokane in the lower

South Hill area. It is constructed like a townhouse with 3 levels. It was the model home, so it has several upgrades the other units do not have, like granite counter tops in the kitchen, one step up cabinets, better faucets in the 2½ bathrooms and a really fancy above counter glass wash bowl in the downstairs bathroom. There are 3 bedrooms. I'm pretty excited about it. I got preapproved for the loan at the bank, and should be moving in around late September or early October. I feel good about this.

I went camping over Labor Day weekend. I went to a place in Long Beach, WA. The camp ground was just a block from the beach. It was a typical RV park, with electricity, water, and cable hookups. The difference was, the owners of this place hosted a cookout on Saturday night, a brunch on Sunday morning, and a potluck on Sunday night. This is most unusual for RV parks, but great fun. I didn't feel alone at all after the cookout. I met lots of the other campers at each of the functions. I had great fun.

On another note, I have been continuing to read "Survivors." In fact I was just reading Chap. 14 and was amazed how well it described my childhood. I was very isolated as a child and have continued to be so into my adulthood. No matter how close I was to people, especially your Mother, I never felt connected in a certain sense. I said many times, "I never understand how you love me" to your Mom. I have always been afraid to get really close to anyone as a friend for fear they would be able to figure out my secret and not want to be my friend anymore. I still have that fear.

Anyway, in this chapter, the author describes his respect and admiration for survivors like me. Despite all the pent up fears and feelings of in-adequacy, I did survive had a somewhat normal existence with a loving family, and finally, more recently a career that was both challenging and satisfying and paid better than any other job I had ever had except as a salesman without the side effect of having to travel. It struck me as an amazing similarity with my own admiration of my Mother's survivor-ship from an abusive marriage and then being able to raise three children by herself, with absolutely no positive input from my father (not capitalized on purpose). Her survival instincts were, in my judgment, were nothing short of phenomenal in the 40's and 50's when divorced women were not generally respected in the community. Mr. Lew says the same thing about survivors like me. He says the fact that I, and others like me, survived to be minimally functional or better is something to be to be admired and praised. I had never thought of my survival in that way. I know this concept is not internalized yet, I but I intend to work on it as a positive way to move on.

I know school is back in session now, so I'm guessing I won't hear from you as much. I hope everything is going well for everyone. Please give my love, hugs, and kisses to Christine, Oliver, and Evan. I love you all very much.

Dad

A Typical RV Park

SO MY FATHER WAS MOVING OUT OF HIS CHEAP APART-ment. Great. But why was he moving into a three-level "model home" condo, with three bedrooms, two-and-a-half bathrooms and granite countertops? Wasn't he living alone? Wasn't this overkill?

But I didn't say anything. I couldn't lament his cheap apart-ment and deride his lavish condo at the same time. Besides, I was sort-of-happy for him. Maybe the fancy condo meant that he thought himself worthy of living in a nice place. He was. Good for him.

I was sort-of-happy, also, that my father was reading the book I sent him and that he was being so candid and thoughtful in his emails. I was sort-of-happy that he might soon be ventur-ing out into "that community" comprised of "male couples." I didn't call my father on his euphemisms, either.

Sometimes, when I felt sort-of-happy for my father, I thought about my mother, about how alone she was and how much she had been duped, and this tempered my sort-of-happi-ness, making this feel less like qualified happiness and more like – What? "Happiness" didn't seem like the right word for any-thing I felt. I was not "happy." I was not, truthfully, even "glad" for my father. I approved. I wanted him to be happy, and I approved of these steps he was taking towards his own happiness, even if they did not make me "happy" or "glad," which is not to say they made me feel worse. Perhaps it's more accurate to say that my father's steps towards happiness – (1) condo-buying and (2) attempting, for the first time in his life, friendships with other gay men – made me complexly aware of my feelings, which were all over an emotional map for which words make lousy coordinates.

Was my father choosing a nice place to live in the hopes that he might someday share this place with others? With friends, with a lover, with a partner? Were those his hopes? I hoped so. I hoped so as long as I didn't at the same time think of my mother.

But there was something fishy about that campground on the Washington coast – the campground in Long Beach – a *typical RV park* with electricity, water, and cable hook-ups. Hosted cookouts, evening potlucks, Sunday morning brunches? Great fun? No loneliness at all? Not that I knew anything about RV parks, but I doubted that your typical RV park would have such a high level of camaraderie. Could it be possible that my father might be keeping something from me? My father? I called him on the phone.

"Hey, Dad, I'm glad you had such a good time on your Labor Day trip."

"I had a really great time," he said. "Fabulous."

I said, "Sounds like you met a lot of nice people."

"Yes."

"A typical RV park," I said.

My father started itemizing: electricity, water, cable hook –

"Dad."

"What?"

"A typical RV park."

My father took a moment before he said, "I think I know where you're going with this."

"Dad, it's a gay campground, isn't it?"

"Gay and lesbian friendly," my father said.

"You're *out*," I said.

My father took this in. "I hadn't thought of it that way. But I guess so. I guess I am. Sort of."

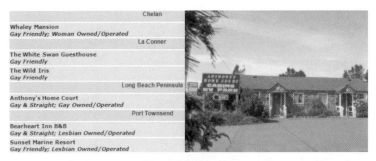

Google search: "campground" and "gay friendly" and "Long Beach, WA"

He told me that there were whole extended families at the campground. There were one and two bedroom cabins. There were little kids. A playground with a sandbox and swings and slides. There were the adult children of gay and lesbian couples who had been coming to this campground for years. It was unlike any place my father had ever been.

"So, basically, your typical RV park," I said.

My father laughed. Then his tone changed completely. "It was the way it should be."

"Amen," I said.

Neither of us said anything for a few moments. I thanked him for his thoughts on the book I'd given him. I asked him when he thought he was going to move into the condo. He was still waiting for the bank approval.

"Where did you find this place?"

"The condo or the campground?"

"The campground."

"On the internet," he said.

"That's great," I said. "I'm happy for you, Dad." And I was, sort of.

To Catch a Thief

MY MOTHER CALLED ME. SHE DIDN'T SAY HELLO. SHE said, "I've changed the locks."

"Why?"

"Your father was in the house."

"He didn't ask to come over?"

"No."

"What did he want?" I knew that my father still had several boxes of things, and some unboxable things, like golf clubs, skis, and his bicycle, in the basement and the garage. My mother wanted him to come and get all this stuff, but so far he hadn't called to arrange a time. My mother didn't want to be there when he picked it all up. It was September. It had been four months since he'd moved out. More than once, my mother had said to me: "If he doesn't come soon, it's all going to be out on the curb with a 'free' sign." My father, it seemed to me, was using his golf clubs, skis, and bicycle to punish my mother for exiling him for a lifetime of betrayal. Classic, post-divorce, bush-league, passive-aggressive antagonism. I didn't want to get in the middle of it. I didn't want to pick sides, even though picking sides wasn't difficult.

My mother said, "He wanted some paperwork in the office, in the filing cabinet. He's moving. He's buying a condo."

"Did he apologize?"

"Words, words, words."

"He didn't get those boxes?"

"He did not."

"I'm sorry, Mom."

"This is not his house anymore. He cannot come and go."

"I know."

"Why would he do that? Why would he want to hurt me more?" she said. "Why wouldn't he ask?"

"I don't know."

"I don't know him."

"I know."

When I got off the phone with my mother, I did not call my father. I did not think, *Robert has recommended anger. Here is another perfect opportunity*. I thought, *Hasn't he hurt her enough?*

A WEEK LATER, my mother called me. She did not say hello. She said, "Your father stole from me."

"No."

"Yes."

"He withdrew three hundred dollars from my bank account." My mother's voice was shaking. I could see her face in my imagination. She was baring her teeth.

"He would never do something like that," I said. What I wanted to say, but didn't, was that my father was the most honest man I knew.

"You don't know him," my mother said.

I CALLED MY father. He picked up. I shouted, "Why did you steal from Mom? You can do whatever you want with your life now, but you cannot hurt her anymore."

"Don't get in the middle of this, son. You don't know –"

"You stole from her," I shouted again.

"I did not steal," my father shouted back. "I took without asking. There's a difference."

I laughed – a derisive, scornful laugh. "That's called stealing."

"No."

"Yes."

I was out on the back patio. The boys gathered at the door. They were leaning into the glass, watching me, like at the aquarium. Christine tried to steer them to other exhibits, but they kept squirming free, running back. I was the best exhibit going. It was just after dinner, an hour or so before dark.

Christine opened the patio door and said, "We're going to the park."

I nodded.

The boys shouted as they were dragged away, "What's the matter? Why is Daddy so angry?"

I told my father that I didn't want to hear his "side of the story." There was no other side of the story. There was only one story, and I understood it well enough. My father did not have enough money in his account to cover the closing costs on his condo. There was a deadline. He went online, entered the user name and password for my mother's account, and he transferred money from her account to his.

My father said that he had *borrowed* the money. He had every intention of paying it back.

"You stole," I said. "Mom has changed the fucking locks. Why? Because you went into her house without asking, when she wasn't there. That's called *breaking and entering*. What the fuck are you doing? What is she going to have to do next? Get a restraining order?"

My father didn't say anything.

"I don't care what your reasons are. I don't want to hear your story. I only care about what you did."

Ten, twenty seconds passed in silence. My father said slowly and clearly, "I don't ever want to speak with you again. I want you completely out of my life." Then he hung up.

I stared at the phone in my hand. I walked around the back patio, my heart pounding, adrenaline coursing through my blood. Mourning doves were calling out from the phone wires above our back fence. The wind was blowing in the trees. The sun was low and red in the Western sky.

My father called back. I let the phone ring. He didn't leave a message.

E-blame

OVER THE NEXT SEVERAL DAYS, MY FATHER AND I LASHED out at each other in a series of long, painful to re-read, recriminating emails:

Me:

When you ask for money from someone, and you are given that money, this is borrowing. When you do not ask for money from someone, but take the money without the other person knowing, this is stealing. Oliver knows this, and he is seven. You and mom taught this to me a very long time ago, and you were both right to do so. There is nothing blurry about this boundary.

My father:

I am incredibly sorry that you are so deeply troubled by the revelation that I am gay and have been for most of my life.

Greg, it seems to me that if we are to have a continuing relationship, you are going to have to stop making demands of me that I cannot meet in this lifetime. I am working on healing what remains of my life and you are not helping. If anything, so far, it appears that you are looking for a reason to write me out of your life because I make you too uncomfortable.

Me:

Your sexual orientation is not what is keeping us apart. So please don't try to oversimplify my reaction by claiming that my problem is that you're gay. It's not. My problem is that you hurt mom again. You made a bad judgment; you also entered her house without her permission, which was also a bad judgment. This hurt her also. When you stop doing things that hurt mom, and when you start seeing that this is the problem, then we'll have clear ground to speak to each other from.

...for you to say that you were justified in being as angry as you were strikes me as coming from a place of deep denial, and an unwillingness to see yourself, and your choices, as the source for this latest round of heartache. And so I just don't find much sympathy in my heart for your denial. I'm weary of your denial and of your refusal to take accountability for your actions. I see you trying to lash out at me rather than look long and hard and humbly at the bad choices you made.

Your ability to justify bad choices must be very powerful – how else could you have kept up such a deceitful life for so very long?

My father:

I am sincerely sorry that I cannot live up to your expectations. If you recall, I've never had the patience to argue with you. I still don't. I'm finished with this line of attacking me. Please write me back when you can move on.

Whitman

IT WAS SATURDAY AFTERNOON IN OCTOBER. I WAS IN front of the television. Outside, it was a bright sunny day, the kind of day that makes people want to live in New Mexico. The kind of day to take your boys to the park. I was watching a PBS documentary on Walt Whitman.

> I am to see to it that I do not lose you
>
> I am faithful
>
> I do not give out
>
> Through me forbidden voices,
> Voices of sexes and lusts, voices veil'd and I remove the veil,
> Voices indecent by me clarified and transfigur'd

CHRISTINE AND THE boys came home from the park. I wasn't the mayor anymore. I had resigned, but without any speech or fanfare. My administration's accomplishments would have to speak for themselves.

Oliver joined me on the futon and watched some of the documentary with me. They had just started talking about Whitman's volunteering as a nurse for the Union during the Civil War. For three years, he lived in a boarding house in D.C. and went to be with the young soldiers for seven or eight hours each day. Sometimes he spent the night sitting in a chair beside them so they would not die alone. Oliver was immediately taken in, fascinated by the black and white grainy photographs of the slain and wounded soldiers, photos of amputated limbs, the burial teams at work, the field hospitals, the surgeons, their rolled-up sleeves and blood-soaked shirts. Whitman wrote in his notebook:

> I do not see that I do much good to these wounded and dying, but I cannot leave them... Most of these sick or hurt are entirely without friend or acquaintances here.

I started to cry. Snot poured out my nose. My mouth was open but no sound was coming out. Oliver left the room and came back with Christine, who sat down beside me and rubbed my back and held me. Oliver was confused. He looked scared. He asked why I was so sad, and when I could finally catch my breath to answer, I said something about how horrible war could be, which was a small part of the truth.

A Well-Made Man

BORN IN 1819, ONE HUNDRED AND TWENTY-
two years before my father, Walt Whitman
became the person he was and invented the person
he became. He cultivated idleness and leisure.
He loafed and invited his soul. He sang the body
electric.

The armies of those I love engirth me, and I engirth them;
They will not let me off till I go with them, respond to them;
And discorrupt them, and charge them with the full charge of the
    Soul. [...]

The expression of the face balks account;
But the expression of a well-made man appears not only in
    his face;
It is in his limbs and joints also, it is curiously in the joints of
    his hips and wrists;
It is in his walk, the carriage of his neck, the flex of his waist
    and knees—dress does not hide him;
The strong, sweet, supple quality he has, strikes through
    the cotton and flannel;
To see him pass conveys as much as the best poem, perhaps
    more;
You linger to see his back, and the back of his neck
    and shoulder-side.

It's a good thing people were so open and affirming in
1855, the year Whitman self-published the first edition of *Leaves*

of Grass. Well, everybody except the most prestigious literary critics of the day. Here are a few excerpts:

> his punctuation is as loose as his morality
> a mass of stupid filth
> natural imbecility
> slimy work
> vile
> intensely vulgar
> absolutely beastly
> an escaped lunatic raving in pitiable delirium
> an explosion in a sewer

Whitman printed 795 copies of *Leaves of Grass*, but he didn't sell thirty. That first year, Whitman gave away more copies than he sold. One reviewer recommended that Whitman be "whipped in the streets"; another recommended that he "commit suicide."

Humility

I WANTED MY FATHER TO KEEP HIS PROMISE TO ME THAT he would never again try to kill himself. I did not want another phone call from – who? Who would call 911 this time? Who would save him? But how could I be sure that my father was keeping his promise if I refused to speak with him? How did I even know he was alive?

I hadn't talked to or emailed with my father in more than four months. I'd gone months without talking to him before, but never out of spite. Thanksgiving had come and gone. Christmas had come and gone, and we did not talk or send each other cards or presents. He did not send the boys presents, either. I added these presents my children did not receive to my litany of grievances. My father didn't have to call or email me, but he could at least send his grandsons presents. In early February, my birthday came and went, and he did not call or write or send anything. He had said that he wanted me out of his life, and I was determined to hold him to it. I am a talented grudge-holder. Except that I wanted him to call and apologize, so that I could then apologize to him. I sometimes went back to those emails he and I had sent in September, about whether or not he was a thief. I could see my own self-righteousness. I had claimed, for example, that I did not shout at him on the phone, that he was the one who was shouting. When I read this again, I laughed. Had I said anything, at any volume, below a shout? I saw also, in my father's emails, his desperation. He was in crisis. I saw my utter lack of sympathy. I saw that not even once did I attempt to ask him, sincerely, why he acted so rashly. He'd always been so incredibly considerate. Had it finally hit him that his life with my mother was over? Was he lashing out against the punishment she had given him. Banishment. A life sentence, without parole. No opportunity for restitution, for redemption. All he could do was pay the penalty. There was nothing he could do to make things right again, not with her. But he could still make things wrong. He could make her acknowledge him, make her feel something for him, even if it was only the pain that came after a lifetime of trust and love, the pain of the love she surely must still have for him.

Maybe that was why. Maybe that had something to do with his motivations, however conscious.

There's a difference between saying, *Why do you think you did that?* And saying, *How could you do that?* Which is not a question but an accusation. Which is another way of saying, *You have forfeited your right to be understood. Shame on you.*

I wanted my father to be the first one to apologize, the humble one.

Man's Best Friend

MY MOTHER'S DOG LUCKY IS NOT A GOOD DOG, THOUGH my mother would tell you otherwise. Lucky is part Australian Shepherd, part barking dog. After my father attempted suicide and moved into a cheap apartment across town, my mother had sole custody of Lucky and decided to take her, once a week for eight weeks, to obedience school. Lucky had perfect attendance but did not earn a certificate. She barked. I visited my mother not long after this, and I could not perceive a difference in Lucky's behavior. She was not, and is not, reformed. Lucky's bark is high and sharp and grating, like claws on a blackboard. She barks to be let outside. She barks when she is outside. She barks to be let back inside. She barks when she is inside and hears something outside. She barks on walks around the block. She barks at the kids on the playground. She barks. I do not like Lucky and I have a hard time keeping this to myself. I am not alone.

My mother's three older sisters are her best friends. After my father attempted suicide and my mother exiled him for life, my mother's sisters began a regular rotation of visiting her. Every other week, one of them was staying at her house, in the guest bedroom, for several days. More than once, they all came together. They are, each of them, in their seventies, and they are still, after all these years, fiercely protective of her. My mother is, and will always be, their baby sister.

When my Aunt Di (on the left in the photo) heard about my father's suicide attempt and the reasons behind it, she

questioned my mother's decision to call 911. She told me that she wished my mother would not have picked up the phone but instead had gone for a long walk. I don't hold this against my Aunt Di. She said this from a place of terrible hurt and terrible empathy. She hasn't changed her mind. I don't hold that against her, either.

Back to Lucky. The winter after my father attempted suicide, my mother drove to Nevada to celebrate both Thanksgiving and then Christmas with her sisters. They would not allow my mother to bring Lucky to their houses. They do not love their baby sister that unconditionally. They made my mother put Lucky in a kennel and come alone.

LUCKY HAS ONLY one eye. The other eye is a gristly socket. In the land of the blind dogs, Lucky would not be queen because of her barking.

My mother hired a local Spokane dog whisperer to come to her home and help her train Lucky. After four or five visits, the dog whisperer diagnosed the problem. My mother was not enforcing her commands. She was not consistent. She forgave Lucky all too easily. She let Lucky bark. The dog whisperer put a shock collar on Lucky, which reduced her to a quivering, whimpering mass of fur. My mother started shouting at the dog whisperer to take the collar off. The dog whisperer shouted back. He could work with Lucky. Lucky was not the problem. The dog was never the problem. It was always the owner. My mother told the dog whisperer to leave this minute and never come back.

My mother said to the dog whisperer, "Get out."

My mother read a dog training book written collectively by an order of monks from outside Saratoga Springs, New York. The Monks of New Skete were semi-famous for raising and training pedigreed German shepherds. My mother loved their book. She recommended it to me. But there was no point in my reading *How to be Your Dog's Best Friend*, because I knew Rocky would always like Christine more than me, and because Rocky had aced obedience school eight years earlier. He was far better behaved than Oliver and Evan, who chewed with their mouths open and farted during dinner without consequence. I went to the library and checked out the monks' *I & Dog* instead. The book is coffee-table-shaped and juxtaposes fine art photographs of monks and dogs amidst pastoral monastery grounds with a series of soulful, dog-based meditations inspired by the Jewish philosopher Martin Buber. Here are some excerpts:

> Dogs are guileless and filled with spontaneity: unlike people, they don't deceive. When we take seriously the words they speak to us about ourselves, we stand face to face with the truth of the matter...
>
> Dogs can spot phoniness a mile away.
>
> Ultimately, dogs enchant us with their honesty, a trait increasingly rare in the nexus of relationships that make up our lives.

My mom took Lucky to the dog park every afternoon. She let Lucky off her leash and then walked the perimeter of the fence enclosure and got some exercise. A couple times a week at this time, she called me on her cellphone. It was a good time to talk because Lucky was too distracted sniffing the other dogs' asses to interrupt our conversation with her barking.

Talking with my mom has always been easy, effortless – even about the hardest of things. A few weeks after my father's suicide attempt, she told me, "Every morning your father put out my vitamins. For years and years. This morning I went down to the kitchen and put my water on for tea, and I said, 'He must have forgot to put out my vitamins.' Then I said, '*You* have to do that now.' Then I realized I was talking to myself."

In telling me this, my mother's tone was animated not by self-pity, but by introspective curiosity. I could almost see this realization added to her mental to-do list: must put out vitamins myself.

We are both quick to laugh, especially about Lucky, who is not smart enough to know her role as my mother's comic foil. My mother insists that Lucky is good-looking. She's always passing on to me other dog owners' compliments on Lucky's good looks. She does this knowing full well that I am unpersuadable. She refuses to acknowledge that these people feel hard pressed to say *something* nice, and they can't just say that Lucky is one of the better-looking one-eyed dogs they've seen.

I did not tell my mother how long it had been since I'd spoken to my father. I did not tell her that he wanted me completely out of his life, that he never wanted to speak to me again. I did not tell her that the game plan was to make him suffer for those words. I didn't like to admit this to myself, and I didn't want to make her feel responsible. Because she would have felt responsible – she would have regretted telling me what he had done, and I didn't want that.

My mother and I talked about the classes we were teaching. Then we talked about whether or not she should retire. She was sixty-eight. I worried about the time, all those hours, my mother would spend alone if she retired. Sometimes I permitted my mother to admit that she was tired. Sometimes I said the right thing. "That's okay, mom. You've been a good soldier for a long time." And she said, "Yes I have." Other times I said the right thing, but my tone indicated otherwise. I was remembering that week after my father's suicide attempt, when I taught her how to run the lawnmower and edger and weed whacker, and I was thinking that these new activities would not take up enough time, and so I was really saying, No. No. No. Chin up. Carry on.

WHEN I TALKED with my mother, I encouraged her to make an appointment and see a counselor. I nagged her relentlessly. Then I suggested that maybe she could take Lucky with her. Lucky might have unresolved trauma from childhood that we didn't know about. Maybe that was what all this barking was about. She wanted to tell us. She was trying to tell us. We just couldn't understand.

"Hate the bark, love the barker," my mother said.

I laughed. I could still count on my mother's black humor. I said, "How about, 'Hate the bark, take the barker to the pound, and get a new dog that doesn't bark except when she's supposed to, like when strange men come to the door'?"

"Or your father," my mother said.

"Sure," I said.

"I think I can train Lucky," my mother said.

"I don't think so," I said.

I cannot understand why this has been so hard for me to initiate this message. I think I've been trying to make it too hard. Only a guess, the first statement stands. I am well, mostly healthy and still working. But I have realized a steady sinking into kind of a depression that is new to me. I've been giving a little thought into how much better it would have been to just not be in this world anymore. I remember promising you that I would not go that route again and I intend to honor that promise. I really believe honoring that promise has prevented me from doing something senseless again. On reflection, there are really more good days than bad days, but those bad days can be really difficult.

On the good side, I recently re-met someone I met several months ago, more in passing than anything else. We are very much alike, having been sexually abused in our youth, but he knew about himself very early and was able to be very open with his family who were very supportive. As a result, I believe he was able to assert himself in the outside world as himself while I never was. As you may remember, I was still in denial for many years after being married. He never married. There is much more I could go on about, but will hold off until I am sure we will really connect for the long term. I kind of hope we do. I am far too cognizant of the troubles that appear to be rampant among gay couples. However, we are neither in our younger years and have a lot of life's experiences behind us, so there is a fair chance for success. We'll see.

I'll close for now. Please give my sincere love to Christine, Oliver, and Evan. I love you very much.

Dad

Accountability

I CALLED MY FATHER AND WE TALKED FOR A FEW MINUTES. We didn't argue the semantics of beg, borrow, or steal. We didn't talk about Thanksgiving or Christmas or my birthday. We didn't talk about how long it had been since we last talked. We didn't talk about his new condo or the new person in his life, with whom he seemed to have much in common. We didn't talk about science fiction or incest self-help literature. We talked about the weather in Spokane and Albuquerque.

Then I said, "I'm sorry you've been having such a hard time lately."

He said, "Thank you, son. I guess it helps to just acknowledge it."

"I think so."

He asked how the boys were doing, and I told him about how, that morning at preschool, Evan and his best friend, Isaac, had been playing on the platform at the top of the slide, and Evan either bumped or pushed Isaac, and Isaac had fallen down the slide headfirst. Isaac's arm was broken; Evan's heart was broken. When I arrived to pick him up after lunch, Evan's face was still flushed red and tear-streaked. When I asked him what happened, he had a hard time catching his breath. He couldn't tell me. His teacher had to tell me. I asked him, "Did you push Isaac? Or was it just an accident?"

Evan didn't answer this question, not then, not later. He just wailed. He kept saying, "I'm so sorry," over and over.

If You Build It

I STARTED IMAGINING A HOUSE IN THE TREES. A TREE-house, in the backyard. There had been talk of a treehouse for a few years. The boys wanted one. I wanted one and wanted to build one. Christine wanted me to build one because the boys wanted one. I just hadn't gotten around to it yet, because of *blah, blah, blah,* and what with *blah, blah, blah.*

My father built a treehouse when I was five or six years old. It wasn't really a treehouse because it was freestanding, but we still called it a treehouse. The top deck was shrouded by branches and leaves. It was in the side yard of the house where I grew up in Lincoln, Nebraska. A host of objects, some harmless, some not, were hurled from the deck down upon suspecting and unsuspecting foes. Headquarters. Refuge. Secret hiding place. The long slow hours of afternoons. Comic books abandoned to weather. The call for dinner. The dark coming on.

IT WAS MARCH, and the days were getting warmer, up into the sixties. Oliver and Evan and I were walking the two blocks to the park in the late afternoons and early evenings. I was capable, again, of ordinary park conversation, so long as you were willing to talk with me about treehouses. I'd bought some lumber and nails and lag bolts and screws. I'd salvaged the two-by-six tongue and groove boards from the old patio cover I'd torn down the year before. The new and salvaged lumber was stacked on the back patio. I had made preliminary notes and sketches but had lost momentum somehow and re-lapsed into the procrastination phase of my creative process.

Dan was a neighborhood dad and an engineer who worked for one of the national laboratories in Albuquerque. He did something with light wave particles, photons maybe. I didn't have the upper division math and physics prerequisites to understand what he did, but I weathered him talking about a recent work project until I could change the subject to treehouses.

It turned out that Dan had built a treehouse a few years before. He mentioned static and dynamic loads. He'd used steel cables set at certain tensions. I said I thought you only used steel cables on suspension bridges and chair lifts at ski resorts. He looked at me and shook his head in the way that engineers always shake their heads at people with MFAs. I told him that I could just about run my tape measure so long as I didn't have to convert fractions.

"I can loan you my blueprints, if you want," he offered.

"You made blueprints?"

Dan had blueprint-making software, which he was willing to loan me as well.

I didn't like blueprints. Like all women her age, Christine wanted a kitchen remodel, and I'd reluctantly glanced at some blueprints in books she'd checked out from the library. I could sometimes tell where the doors were. Nothing left me dizzy like blueprints. They never became three dimensional holograms, like the intercepted plans for the Death Star do at the end of *Return of the Jedi*.

"Maybe you could just write a story about a treehouse?" Dan said unkindly.

"About not building a treehouse after all," I said, "about giving up and failing my children and myself?"

"Right," Dan said. "Isn't failure one of the writer's great subjects?"

"Engineers aren't supposed to know that," I said.

I left the park demoralized. I couldn't even pretend to be alpha male of the neighborhood. Not with guys like Dan in the pack. Or Steve, an ER doctor with a beat-up truck and a motorcycle. I drove a twelve-year-old Saturn station wagon. Travis used to race mountain bikes professionally. My mountain bike didn't have a suspension fork. DJ drank more than anyone else on poker nights but never seemed drunk and consistently won big. Mark was a teacher, like me, but he'd climbed a bunch of the fourteeners in Colorado. You didn't get points towards alpha male by coming up with the best similes. They deducted points from the guy with the best similes. I'd been hoping that my treehouse would move me up in the standings, but there was no way my treehouse would be better than Dan's. His treehouse probably had a wall made entirely of glass, cantilevered at an architecturally sophisticated angle. His treehouse probably had an elevator that opened onto an atrium.

ONE EARLY WEEKEND morning, right after coffee, I put Dan mostly out of my mind. I went outside into the cool spring air and got after it. I nailed together the two-by-six floor joists. The platform was to be eight feet by nine feet. I wanted one of the branches of the tree to come up through the floor of the treehouse deck and another branch to support the platform. The rest would be supported by four-by-four posts set into holes dug three feet deep.

Out in the yard, I hammered wooden stakes in the ground where the postholes would be and ran a string between them to make sure the corners were true. I stood in the space between the strings and looked up to see where the branch of the tree would pass through the deck. This eyeballing wasn't precise enough. In a moment of inspiration, I tied a one-half inch hex nut to a long piece of string and dropped this string from the tree branch. A plumb line! My stakes were in the right place! I went inside for a second breakfast to thunderous imaginative applause.

When I came out Evan was jumping around in the grass

inside the strings. He was in his pajamas. My hex nut plumb line had become a pendulum.

"Look, Dad," Evan said. "I'm playing in the treehouse!" And he was. The treehouse in Evan's mind was real in the way memory is real, like the memory I have now of that time before I built a treehouse. Igor Stravinsky says in *Poetics of Music*: "Invention presupposes imagination but should not be confused with it ... What we imagine does not necessarily take on concrete form and may remain in a state of virtuality; whereas invention is not conceivable apart from its actually being worked out."

Stravinsky says, "We have a duty towards music; namely, to invent it."

I had begun to feel Stravinskian about the treehouse, a deep inner obligation, a faith that it would not be just Evan and Oliver who needed the treehouse, but other children in the neighborhood as well, children known to me and not yet known. I felt that my neighborhood itself would be a better place because of the treehouse. I had a duty towards treehouses; namely, to build one.

Evan ran around inside the strings for a while. When he went back in the house, I cut the strings and where each stake had been, I dug a deep hole. The first foot and half went quickly; the next foot and a half took ten times as long – the soil deeper down was hard clay, but it broke up in small pieces if I just kept chipping away at it. This was a metaphor if I wanted one, but I didn't. I didn't want a post hole digger, either. Steve had one, but I didn't want to ask anyone for anything or tell anyone what I was up to. Not anymore. I was all through with talk. I felt like working hard. My self-pity had melted away. I felt purposeful, attentive, focused.

At the bottom of each of these holes I set a brick. I carried the floor joist platform over from the patio and set it on the ground so that each posthole was now in a corner of the frame.

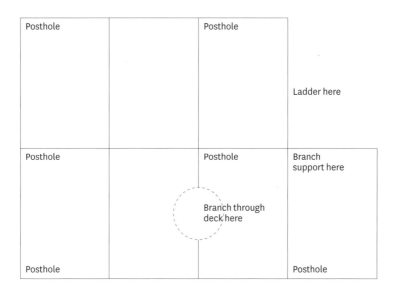

In a feat of mechanical advantage that would have made Archimedes proud, using two thin ropes each running through pulleys set high up in the tree, Oliver and Evan and I hoisted the platform slowly into the air. We tied off the ropes. The frame of the floor of our treehouse swayed in the breeze above our heads. There was cheering. Christine came out to see what was going on, and she could not quite disguise her pride in her man.

One by one we set the posts in their holes, and by inserting lag bolts through pre-drilled holes, we connected each post to the platform six feet off the ground, leaving the nuts only finger-tight, for now. We'd tighten them later, when the posts were plumb. In discussion threads all over the internet, the question of setting posts has been examined. Ready-mix concrete or compressed soil? I based my decision on the terse conviction of a Wyoming rancher. His ranch was big; he maintained a lot of fence; he couldn't pour concrete in all those holes. Compress the soil, he said. It works.

Christine used the level to make sure each post was plumb, and with a two-by-two, Oliver and Evan I took turns tamping the dirt we kicked back in the holes. It worked and still works. Those posts ain't going nowhere.

We untied the ropes and pulleys. We didn't need them anymore.

The boys wanted to get up on the frame and walk on the open joists, balance beam style. This wasn't particularly safe, but I got my ladder and propped it against the frame. I went up and Oliver and Evan followed. Maternal exhortations reached us faintly from somewhere far below. The boys started out on their knees. Then they stood, holding on to the tree's branch coming up through the joists. I was happy. The boys were happy. Christine was unhappy. The boys and I stayed up there a good while, growing more confident, but never just walking out with our arms outspread. The day was ending. We came down the ladder. I cleaned up the site and put my tools away. Christine made hot dogs and french fries, and we ate dinner out on the patio and looked at the frame of the floor of our house in the trees.

The next morning, I nailed and set the salvaged two-by-six tongue and groove flooring. This went fast. I left only a few inches between the emerging branch of the tree and the deck flooring, and so now when the wind blows hard, the branch sways, and the whole treehouse creaks and groans satisfyingly. The boys climbed the ladder onto the finished platform and looked around, feasting their eyes about. They could see down into each of the neighbor's yards – north, south, and west.

The boys went back inside. I built the stud walls of the house with the two-by-sixes that I ripped into two-by-fours. I didn't own a table saw or a chop saw, and so I did all this cutting and ripping on my Porter Cable circular saw. If I were willing to advertise this, it would certainly earn me points towards alpha male of the neighborhood. My guess was that Dan had more power tools than Norm Abram on New Yankee Workshop. I was practically a Shaker by comparison. But I kept all this to myself. I didn't care about that anymore. I screwed in one-by-ten pine boards for siding, leaving windows all around. I notched and nailed rafters. I nailed down the pine board roof. I built a wrap-around picket railing.

Mark donated a yellow slide which had once been con-nected to a five foot high playfort that he'd torn down a few years before. I attached the slide to the six foot high deck of the tree-house. I didn't think the one foot difference would matter much. But early tests involving my real children proved otherwise. Gravity took on new meaning for them. No bones were broken. I built a stand which raised the bottom of the slide eighteen inches off the ground. This was better. But the yellow slide is still not without peril. There is a steep learning curve to sticking the land-ing, especially for toddlers.

Evan and I hung a pulley to a branch of the desert willow, just off the deck of the treehouse. We ran a thin, nylon rope through the pulley and connected it at the bottom to a pale blue Easter basket. The basket is light so if it falls on someone's head, it won't crack their skull open.

ONE AFTERNOON, NOT long after I built the treehouse, I came home from work and the house was strangely quiet. Evan was playing with magnets on the living room rug. Christine was stand-ing with her arms crossed in our bedroom, staring at the wall.

Oliver had yelled at her. She always took Evan's side. Where was
Oliver? She didn't know.

I had an idea where Oliver might be. I went out the back
door into the yard and climbed the ladder up into the treehouse.
I ducked inside the doorframe and sat next to him. He didn't
look angry, which was what I expected. He sat cross-legged, his
elbows on his knees, his head in his hands.

"You look pretty sad," I said.

He didn't answer. He put his hand on my arm. I have a
small mole on the inside crook of my elbow, and he found it and
started worrying it with his index finger. He had been doing
this since he was a baby. I didn't particularly like the way it felt,
but he'd been doing it so long, it was too late to stop him now.
I'd never called his attention to it.

Oliver looked tired. He and Evan had been staying up too
late, sometimes past ten, talking in their bunkbeds, giggling,
goofing around. Last night Oliver was telling Evan that you don't
want to join the army if your name is Will. Sooner or later, the
captain is going to say, "Fire at Will." Evan got the joke immediately. He was still repeating, "Fire at Will" and giggling after
Oliver had fallen asleep.

We sat together quietly for a while. The sun had gone down.
The backyard was in shadow, and it was dark under the roof of
the treehouse.

Finally Oliver said, "I felt like just going away, but I
decided to come up here."

NO DISCUSSION OF the treehouse could be complete without
mentioning chihuahuas. Our neighbors to the north have three
chihuahuas, and they bark their collective yippie-dog ferocious
bark whenever anyone even thinks about climbing up the
ladder to the treehouse. Evan discovered that if he blew bubbles
out the window of the treehouse so that they floated lazily over
the stuccoed wall, this would render the chihuahuas apoplectic.

Subject:

Date: Thu, 13 Mar 2008

Hi Greg,

I hope everyone is well in your household by now. I had a bad bump on my nose about 3 weeks ago that is well healed, but was really ugly for a while. I was helping my friend fix a piece of plastic corrugated roofing that had pushed through the carport from the weight of two feet of snow when the ladder slipped out from under me and I dropped straight down onto a plastic trash can. Luckily the lid was on it or I probably would have cut my nose severely. I had a big scab for about two weeks. I'm fine now, thank goodness.

My life appears to have settled out a bit and getting more comfortable. I have met a couple of other people that are just good friends to hang out with on weekends. This is much better than sitting at home alone watching TV or playing games on the computer.

I had laser surgery on my right eye today to clear off a small film of cells that have grown on my artificial lens. I am surprised at how much difference it made in my vision after the dilation wore off. I will have the left eye done next Thursday.

MomMom is continuing to decline. I know from my own work with people with her condition that she has nowhere to go but down. I just hate to see it. When I saw her last June, she was so frail and had such a weak voice and I had to cry when I got off by myself. The thought has occurred to me that someday you may have to see your Mom and I in just such a condition. It was a sobering thought. I didn't like it very much. I suppose you could say you have already seen me in worse condition. I personally would hope that it never happen again.

Enough of that. I would like to try to fly down for a weekend sometime when it is convenient for you and the family. I haven't seen Christine and the kids in too long a time. I hope I can get an invite.

Will close for now. Love you all very much.

Dad

Invitation

I WANTED TO INVITE MY FATHER TO VISIT. I WANTED TO see him again, and I wanted Christine and the boys to see him. But I balked. For days I didn't respond to my father's email. I didn't understand my reluctance. Hadn't I just built a treehouse? Wasn't I all better? A week went by. I knew this wasn't okay. Even though I could easily explain (lie) that I just hadn't checked my email in a while, I knew that my father would be checking his email regularly for my answer, and each day that passed with no response would confirm his fear. On some level I must have known that seeing my father again, in my own home, and that my children seeing him again, would mark a change in the nature of our relationship, an acceptance on my part of things as they were, an acceptance of him that was more than words. The end of one time, and the beginning of another.

Not just acceptance but one more step towards forgiveness.

The poet Richard Hugo wrote, "No two hurts are the same and most have compensations / too lovely to leave."

Oliver, Evan, and I spent the night in the treehouse. New Mexico nights in the middle of March are not warm. There was still lots of snow in the mountains. Concerns about hypothermia were dismissed. We'd survive. We had sleeping bags rated to fifteen degrees. We had air mattresses and pillows. We had winter hats and flannel pajamas. We had books and headlamps. I snuck up candy bars, using the pulley basket. I said, "Now, whatever you do, don't tell mom."

"MOM," Evan screamed. "MOM! Come. You've got to come."

Christine came out into the backyard. She looked pretty in the glow of light from the kitchen.

"You'll never believe what Daddy did," Evan said.

"What did he do now?" Christine's hands were on her hips.

"He snuck us candy bars. Using the PULLEY BASKET!"

"It's true," I admitted.

"I'm going to have to spank your Daddy," Christine said, and she went back into the house.

"Thanks a lot, Evan," I said.

"You knew I would tell," Evan said.

"I thought you might."

I told the boys a story, one of my originals, about Trixie the Adventure Cat, her roommate Bobo the Dog, and the alley rats, Max, Perkins, and Raoul. Trixie and Bobo lived in a modest bungalow. Out in the alley lived Max and his notorious gang. Max and the rats were always sneaking into Trixie's house, stealing things, playing pranks – causing mischief and mayhem. Tonight, Trixie and Bobo were trying to get to sleep in their brand new treehouse, but the alley rats kept making ghostly noises from somewhere below. A note was mysteriously pulled up to Trixie and Bobo in the pulley basket. Beware.

Evan said, "I'm scared. I think I heard something. I want to go inside and sleep with Mommy."

I told Evan it was time to be brave. He could do it.

Evan must have heard something in my voice, because he said, "Okay, Daddy. I can be brave."

After the story, after the boys had gone quiet and were settled in their sleeping bags, I sat up and said, "I want to ask you guys something."

They looked at me, their eyes shining in the dark.

"What do you think about Grandpa coming to visit?"

They both said, "Yeah!" at once. Evan said, "Do you think Grandpa would want to spend the night in the treehouse?"

"I don't know if he'd go for that," I said.

"That's okay," Evan said.

The stars came out. The boys fell asleep. I stayed up for a long time listening to all the night sounds near and far – Rocky wandering the yard below, unable to climb up the ladder and join us, his collar and tags jangling softly; planes in the distance flying south toward the airport; the train blowing its horn as it passed through downtown.

~~~~~~

Subject: **RE:**

Date: Sun, 23 Mar 2008

Hi Greg,

Thank you for the invitation to come for a visit. I have already told my boss that I will be off for the trip. I'll let you know about the flight times as soon as I know something. I'm really looking forward to seeing you all again. It has been too long since I've seen Christine and the boys.

Thanks so much for your very supportive remarks. I cannot express how warm it makes me feel to know that you can continue to accept me under very different circumstances. I am beginning to not feel so isolated. It is nice to have friends that I can call just to chat and visit socially. I am reminded of how social I was a long time ago. For the past more-than-several years, I have only had social friends who were related to your Mom's work friends. As more time goes by, I feel sure I will become very comfortable with my social environment and have a much more active life outside the house.

About the tree house, I really do wish I could have been there for the construction. It was a lot of fun for us to see you playing in our yard with your friends. From a practical point of view, it was a real plus to know exactly where you were, as well. Also, I hope you will share your plans for the kitchen remodel with me. As you may remember, I was the top designer/salesman in the kitchen-bath design department for all of Hechinger's 126 stores when we were in Northern Virginia.

With luck, I might be able to offer some practical suggestions for the space you have and about the specific features you may want.

I'll close for now. Love you very much.

Dad

First Person Plural

MY FATHER CAME TO VISIT FOR A LONG WEEKEND OVER Evan's fifth birthday, in April. In the days before he came, I felt strangely fragile, almost sick to my stomach with nerves. When the boys and I picked him up from the airport, they threw themselves into his arms, laughing and shouting and talking at the same time, and he picked them up and bear-hugged them, and it was as if something broke open inside my chest, and I had to walk away for a minute because tears were streaming down my face. We drove home together in the car, then walked to the park with the boys. Later we sat at the kitchen table together and ate dinner. But I didn't know how to talk to him – not around the boys, not in those moments when we would find ourselves alone together. I didn't know how to tell him how awful those grudge-filled months were when we didn't talk to one another. I didn't know how to acknowledge this to myself, much less to him, without self-pity, without lacing my words with blame and bitterness. I didn't want him to be forever defensive and apologetic. And so, contrary to my character, during those four days of my father's visit, I was mostly quiet.

Christine took lots of photos, because it was Evan's birthday, and maybe because she knew how much my father's visit mattered to me, and to him. My father in his sweatpants and Coca-cola t-shirt and uncombed thinning hair helping Evan open his presents at 6:30 in the morning. My father on his knees on the floor helping Evan put together one of his new Lego sets. Evan sitting in my father's lap as my father reads Evan one of his new books. My father, later, at Evan's birthday party, off to the side, as Evan plays with his friends from the neighborhood and from preschool. My father standing in our unremodeled kitchen eating pizza with the parents of Evan's friends. In these pictures, my father appears content, happy, at ease.

My father kept speaking in the first person plural.

I was walking through kitchen, and I heard him say to my neighbor Andrew, "We took one of those cruises to Alaska one summer." I kept going. That trip he took with my mom to Alaska was more than ten years ago. Another time, on my way back through the kitchen, my father was talking to Tom now. Tom and Amy had just remodeled their kitchen. It was mostly their fault that we had to remodel ours now. My father said to Tom, "We've lived in so many places. I don't know how many houses we've remodeled. It seems like a dozen." I stopped and looked at him. He said, "Hey, Son. I don't know how many rooms we painted white over the years."

I didn't say anything.

Then he said to Tom, "Greg's mother didn't like purple rooms or blue rooms or whatever kind of color people think of to paint a room."

I nodded. This was true enough. I took scissors from the drawer. I needed to go hang the piñata.

Twenty minutes later I went out to the backyard and my father was talking to Gerhardt, Isaac's dad. They were both looking up at Evan and Isaac in the treehouse. Isaac had yet to go down the dangerous yellow slide. Isaac's arm was still in its cast. Gerhardt appeared unconcerned. He was giving my father his attention. My father said, "That's what everyone told us, but we did it anyway."

I didn't know what they were talking about. The danger of treehouses? The danger of having children who will someday judge your every stray word?

There was that "we" again. I wanted to sidle up to my father

and say, as blithely as possible, "Dad. They know. They know
you're divorced. They know you're gay. They know you attempted
suicide. I was gone last summer for two-and-a-half weeks.
They know the whole goddamn thing. There is no more *we*." But
I didn't. It helped that there were too many people around –
children and adults – who were having fun. I didn't demand that
my father refrain from any implication that he was still a married man, that he had any ongoing relationship with my mother.
I wanted to say these things, but instead, I walked away.

I found Christine in the living room. She was adjudicating
a dispute over Nerf swords between three of Evan's friends.
There were only two swords. Turns would have to be taken.

I interrupted. "My father keeps saying, *we*, as in 'We
loved it when the neighborhood kids came over to play in the
treehouse.'"

Christine said, "If you want one of these swords, you'll
have to wait your turn."

I didn't laugh or smile. I didn't even say, "Can't I just take
one? I'm bigger." That's only what occurs to me to say now. Then,
I didn't say anything. I was too focused on making myself crazy
over the word *we*.

My father laughed and smiled. Over the three hours of
the party, he worked the different rooms of the house – kitchen,
dining room, living room. He mingled in the front yard and
on the back patio. My father had been so alone for almost a year,
and it was clear that he simply enjoyed being in the company
of people who had only goodwill in their hearts toward him, who
never once betrayed to him their knowledge of the tragic turns
his life had taken, who laughed and smiled when he laughed and
smiled, who clapped him on the shoulder and listened to him
talk about the treehouse he'd built all those years ago, who
listened to his ideas for our kitchen remodel, who listened to him
make all kinds of references to the ordinary happy life he and
his wife had shared and, by the sound of it, still shared. Not one
of them put him on the spot or called him out. No one said,

"Where is she? Where's Evan's grandma? Could she not make it for some reason?" Not one of them came up to me later and said, "It was like your father was talking in his sleep, and I didn't want to wake him."

It is so much easier in retrospect to see that afternoon with charity – charity towards my father, and towards my own difficulty. What was my father supposed to say? "Hey, it's really good to talk to you, because I've been really lonely since I attempted suicide! Because, you know what? I got divorced after that, because I'm gay! Oh, and by the way, my father molested me for over ten years of my childhood!" Wouldn't that have been a lot like what I was doing to some of these very same people at the park only months before, assaulting them with my unfiltered, raw emotion?

Was my father lying to himself and, however casually, to people he'd just met who had no stake in his description of his life? I don't know. I don't think so. And I don't really care. Not now. What was he supposed to do – deny all those years of happiness with my mother? His understanding of those years had not changed. It was only her understanding, and my understanding, that had changed. He had known all along. Was he now not supposed to even mention my mother? What were the rules? Who established them? Wasn't it true that his use of the first person plural was a combination of lifelong habit and more poignantly his longing, still and always, for my mother? Why couldn't I hear this in every word he was saying?

It should have been no surprise to me that my father would not burden anyone with his problems. It would have been absolutely inappropriate and self-absorbed for him to make the parents of Evan's friends uncomfortable with his story, with *total honesty*, whatever that means.

IT IS A Cooney-Martin birthday boy tradition to have one of those inflatable jumping castles in the front yard. This time, it was a Scooby-Doo jumping castle. I can't remember taking my

shoes off, crawling inside, and jumping around wildly, causing pandemonium and screaming, though that is something I'm fond of doing. I can't remember if my father got in the jumping castle and jumped around, though that is the kind of thing he would do, also.

I think back to my father's first visit to my home after his suicide attempt and revelation, and a part of me wants to say that nothing really happened. The boys didn't once ask their Grandpa about his divorce from Granny. They did not ask him why? Was it because this no longer occurred to them to ask? Or could they sense, as if it were a scent in the air, that this was not a subject he wanted to talk about? Not once did I talk with my father about what his life was like as a divorced, gay man. I didn't ask him about his trip to Long Beach, Washington, to the gay-friendly campground that was not a typical RV park. I didn't ask if he was still seeing the man he'd written about in his email. Throughout his visit, I was frustrated with myself for what I took to be my lack of courage, for my failure to engage my father at a deeper level, but now I'd like to take this opportunity to congratulate myself for just letting my father be.

It was not an uneventful visit. It's not true that nothing

happened. My sons spent four happy days with their grandpa. My father spent four happy days with his grandsons, with me, and with Christine, who was unfailingly kind, warm, interested in whatever it was my father wanted to talk about – the layout of his condo, an elderly patient who was too far gone for my father to help, the nerve pain running down his leg, and the medicine he took which gave him constipation. Sometimes I listened, and sometimes I busied myself in other parts of the house. Long before my father's unspeakable revelation, I had lost patience with his penchant for talking about dietary fiber and the consistency of his bowel movements. We played Scrabble. We played Go Fish. We went out to breakfast and dinner. We went bowling, with rails along the gutters, and Evan shoved his six-pound ball with two hands down the lane, and we all watched it roll ever-so-slowly toward the pins.

I was neither happy nor sort-of-happy. But I welcomed my father into my home, and I did not fuck things up. I wanted to – for four days, the desire to fuck things up was like a slow leak hissing out my pores. I wanted to shout, over and over, *It should not be like this! Mom should be here! I hate* – But I did not. I did not even sigh or scowl. My bitterness lost.

I drove my father to the airport. I got out and pulled his bag from the back and set it on the curb and we gave each other a hug, and I said, "I'm really glad you came."

"I am, too," he said. "I want to come again in June, for Oliver's birthday."

"Definitely," I said, and watched him roll his bag through the sliding doors and disappear.

As I drove home, it came to me that my father could not give me what I really wanted, which was to restore to me my previous understanding of our relationship. In the old understanding, it never mattered to me how existentially forthcoming he was. I just liked being around him. I liked the sound of his laugh – a booming, spontaneous laugh that sometimes caught me off guard. Very few people I have known are as companionable.

Compliments, praise – they come easy for him. There was, and is, nothing begrudging about him. My father was always saying things like, "That's just great" and "You know, I think you're right about that" and "I hadn't thought of it that way before." He made people feel smart, funny, valued. He made me feel that way.

I can see now that, for me, the drama of my father's visit was interior, marked by my struggle to discern what silences were acceptable, by my recognition of my ongoing unhappiness with the way things were, by the absence of melodrama, by the effort of will to allow my father to spend time with us without the threat of constant reckoning, by the desire to not inflict more damage, to not make things worse, to not pile hurt onto hurt like wood on a pyre.

Pop-Up Tent Trailer

MY FATHER VISITED AGAIN, IN THE MIDDLE OF JUNE, FOR Oliver's eighth birthday. He drove down from Spokane with his pop-up tent trailer hitched to the ball mount of his SUV. The day after Oliver's party, we all went camping in the Pecos Wilderness, to one of my favorite spots on the planet – a high alpine meadow above 9,000 feet along the Santa Barbara River. My father, the boys, and I put up the pop-up tent trailer, while Christine watched from a camper chair, unmesmerized by our manly competence. We went for a hike. Rocky won the award for happiest mammal. We gathered firewood and made a fire. We roasted marshmallows and made s'mores. We all slept in the pop-up tent trailer, which the boys thought was far better than sleeping in a tent, and this has ever since prejudiced their experience of camping with their minimalist father.

I did not fuck this visit up, either.

The Way We Were

EVAN IS WANDERING THE HOUSE IN A FUNK. HE'S NOT himself. He's not running from the front door to the hallway and back, gesturing, talking to himself, narrating, singing, daydreaming in motion.

Evan comes into the kitchen and stands there looking lost. Christine says, "What's the matter, sweetheart?" Evan sighs. "I miss our old refrigerator."

"I know," Christine says. "Change is really hard. You wish that things could have stayed the same, don't you?"

"I never asked for this *new, fancy* refrigerator. I liked our old one better."

I knew exactly how Evan felt.

DURING THE ENDLESS summer of the Cooney-Martin kitchen remodel, our small 1970s white refrigerator, which came with the house when we bought it, was relocated to the living room, along with the kitchen table and the microwave. Evan liked this. It was like camping in your own living room, with your own refrigerator. But then one day when he came home from a friend's house, there was a brand spanking new, stainless steel Whirlpool Gold, Energy-Star, bottom drawer freezer refrigerator in the kitchen, and the old white refrigerator was out by the curb. Evan struggled with this. He howled. He held a vigil, lasting into the dark of evening and past bedtime, out on the curb beside the old refrigerator. He crumpled the "Free" sign Christine had taped on the refrigerator and threw the ball of paper in the middle of the street.

The next morning, Evan woke up and went outside and sat beside the refrigerator in his yellow SpongeBob pajamas. He brought out his collapsible Buzz Lightyear lawn chair and set it on the sidewalk. It was a sit-in, a non-violent protest that could only make his mother proud, even though she hated the old white refrigerator, which I thought was perfectly fine. She loved her new stainless steel refrigerator more, at that particular time and perhaps still, than she loved me.

People passing by slowly in their cars stopped to look at the old white, beloved refrigerator.

"Hi there," they said sweetly to Evan. "Are you giving away your refrigerator?"

"No!" Evan snarled. "You can't have it."

The people drove away.

Mark walked over. He had a daughter in high school and was unmoved by Evan's unhappiness. He wanted the refrigerator. He could come get it right now. He had his own handtruck but rarely had such a fine occasion to put it to use. He could just wheel the refrigerator down the street. Evan watched this conversation transpire with growing disbelief.

"Hey, Evan," I said. "Mark's the one who gave us the yellow slide for the treehouse."

Tears were streaming down Evan's face. He hopped up and down. His whole face turned red. He was crying his hardest, giving his full effort, which is all you can really ask for.

Mark said, "Evan. Wait. Stop. Listen. I have a deal for you." He had to say this a few times before Evan could hear over the tantrum he was throwing. Finally Evan stopped, his fists balled at his sides.

"What if," Mark said, "I just *borrow* the refrigerator from you, since you don't have room for it anymore. I'll borrow it and keep it in my garage. And that way I can put beer and soda and stuff in there for me, but I'll always keep a few juice boxes in there for you, and you can come down and visit your refrigerator any time you want. You'll just come over and say, 'Hey, Mark, how is my refrigerator doing?' And I'll say, 'Just great, Evan. You want a juice box? I've been keeping one cold for you?' And then you can have one if your mom and dad say it's okay. How does that sound?"

A smile slowly emerged on Evan's face. This smile grew wider. Then Evan jumped up and raised his fist in victory. He shouted, "Yeah!"

Mark looked at me.

I said, "Sure."

"I can come visit my refrigerator?" Evan said.

"Any time. And you can have a juice box when you visit," Mark added. "You can come down for a juice box later today. It won't take me long to get it all set up. Okay?"

"Okay," Evan said. "Yes. Okay." He wiped his tear-stained cheeks with the backs of his hands and wiped them on his shirt. He grinned mischievously. "Can my Dad have one of your beers?"

"He can, Evan. There's gotta be some kind of game on. You could both come in for a while and watch TV."

"Awesome," Evan said. He wandered off to play with his toys. He didn't even watch the refrigerator roll down the street.

Dear Oliver and Evan,

I know you've been worried for some time about Master. I have shared your concern. Please know that I've been keeping my eyes upon him, especially in the mornings before you and The Beloved One awake. Master is up so early that I don't even need to urinate. Not badly, anyway. But I go out and urinate on the tree and the lilac bush, because I know that our routine helps Master feel better. I don't scratch on the door to be let back in, because I know he does not like this. I wait. I am patient. Sometimes he forgets about me, and after a while, I whine, once, twice, not loudly, I do not bark, for I do not want to wake The Beloved One. Master hears and lets me in and we sit together in the dark of the morning time.

I wanted to tell you that I think Master is getting better. He has started to write on his laptop in the mornings, and this can only be for the good. I know The Beloved One shares this feeling. I heard her say this to the telephone when Master was away.

I will close now, but wanted to bring you these tidings.

Yours in deepest loyalty,

Rocky

Hypotheticals

IN THAT PBS DOCUMENTARY ON WALT WHITMAN, ED FOLSOM gets my vote for most valuable featured expert. He's incredibly learned, but also completely engaged – Whitman's life and troubles and poetry and journals are so alive to him, so crucial, relevant, contemporary. Folsom's voice becomes trance-like, incantatory, he is so worked up about Whitman's capacity to identify with complete strangers:

> How do you come to care for people that you have never seen before and that you may never see again? Every day we encounter people, eyes make contact, we brush by people, physically come into contact with them, and may never see them again. But Whitman's notebooks at this time are filled with images, just jottings, of these people, what they're doing, what they look like, what their names are. 'What is this person doing? What's the activity that defines this person? If I were doing that activity that person would be me. If I were wandering the other way, rather than this way, that person could be me. That could be me. That could be me. What is it that separates any of us?'

…That could be me. That could be me. That person could be me.

I'd been doing some hypothetical speculation, myself, on my father's behalf. If only my father would have gone there or done that, he could have been … If he'd read *Leaves of Grass* when he was a young man … If he'd moved to Greenwich Village or San Francisco after high school instead of to an even more rural Virginia, to Blacksburg, a small town in the heart of Appalachia …

But Whitman never thinks this way. Whitman does not

identify with complete strangers so that he can imagine a do-over. He identifies out of fascination and curiosity and empathy and the transcendental belief that our separation from one another is not nearly so distinct as it seems.

Whitman does not identify with the slave on the auction block out of sour grapes over his own fate. Whitman says, That could be me.

Whitman is as audacious as he is sincere as he is determined. With all people, of all races and ethnicities and sexual orientations and professions and heritages, in catalog after catalog in his long-lined, loose-limbed verse, Whitman is saying, This is who we are. All of us. This is who *I* am. That could be me.

I can't say when I stopped posing hypotheticals on behalf of my father. But at some point I began to understand a number of different things at once. I understood that not one of my hypotheticals could have helped my father feel better about himself at his core. Not *Leaves of Grass*. Not a walk-up in the Village or an apartment in the Castro. I could not restore to my father something he'd never had. My father was molested before he could read or write. He needed more help than a book or any liberal, progressive locale could provide. He needed a different father.

I understood also that every one of my better-case scenarios inexorably lead to the same end: if my father had been truly different in the ways I was imagining, he would not have married my mother, he would not have become my father, and I would not exist. I would not have grown up to marry Christine and be a father to my sons. This is basic, obvious. Science Fiction 101. Mess with the chain of causality and everything changes. My life *depended* on my father's shame and denial and secret life. My life, and the lives of my sons, *depended* on thousands of years of bigotry and hate-filled fear-mongering that was only now, in our lifetimes, beginning to change. When my father was leaving adolescence and entering adulthood, in the late fifties, Ellen did not have her own show. There were no openly gay cowboys on *Bonanza*, not even clichéd, limp-wristed, flamboyant

 ones. We were alive, my sons and I, because my father looked at his future and all its possibilities, and thought: Here is a path to happiness. *Marriage. Fatherhood. If only I can just not… If only I can just be …*

I didn't want a different father. I wanted to find a way to love my father the way I had always loved him. But that was no longer possible. I would have to find new ways to love him, to go along with the old ways that remained.

Subject: **CDs & Article**

Date: Tue, 21 Oct 2008

Hi Greg,

I received your package and the article. Thank you so much. I have played two of the CDs so far and really love them. I will load up to five in my car and be able to listen to them when going places, like next weekend on my trip to Long Beach and the Halloween party at Anthony's. I have been looking forward to receiving them and have been really pleased with what I've heard so far. I will enjoy them a lot for a long time…

I have been getting out in the evening a little more of late. There are a couple of local bars where gay people congregate and both have Karaoke nights on Mondays and Wednesdays. I really enjoy singing along while others take the stage. I've even sang a few songs myself. However, most of the other singers do more recent stuff, and I have a tendency to stick to the material I know, like folk music. Please don't worry that I am drinking too much. I don't. I usually have one drink then move to soft drinks or water. I know there is still a possibility of becoming an alcoholic since my dad was. There is also the fact that alcoholics have a tendency to become diabetics and I surely want to avoid that. Besides, that's just not me.

I've been working a little more lately. It looks like the business is picking up on a steady basis. My boss is almost ready to expand to Seattle. He will go there and I will stay here in Spokane. We have already expanded into Coeur d'Alene and making plans to expand down toward the Tri Cities. This is something I could do for many years.

I love you all very much. Thanks again for the CDs and the magazine.

Dad

Walt Whitman (seated, collar open, shirt unbuttoned at the neck, chair back on two legs) at Pfaff's, a bar where gay people congregate in lower Manhattan. 1857.

My Father Contains Multitudes

THE PSYCHOLOGIST PAUL BLOOM DOESN'T SUBSCRIBE to the traditional view of the self, in which "a single, long-term-planning self – a you – battles against passions, compulsions, impulses, and addictions." He offers instead a model of the first person plural:

> The idea is that instead, within each brain, different selves are continually popping in and out of existence. They have different desires, and they fight for control – bargaining with, deceiving, and plotting against one another ... struggles over happiness involve clashes between distinct internal selves ... Some members are best thought of as small-minded children – and we don't give 6-year-olds the right to vote. Just as in society, the adults within us have the right – indeed, the obligation – to rein in the children. In fact, talk of "children" versus "adults" within an individual isn't only a metaphor; one reason to favor the longer-term self is that it really is older and more experienced. We typically spend more of our lives not wanting to snort coke, smoke, or overeat than we spend wanting to do these things; this means that the long-term self has more time to reflect. It is less selfish; it talks to other people, reads books, and so on. And it tries to control the short-term selves. It joins Alcoholics Anonymous ... and sees the therapist ... The long-term, sober self is the adult.

But what if the long-term, reflective adult self has spent most of his life in existential confusion? What if it is only the child who is impulsive, deceptive, but let's also say courageous enough, to be gay? How does the adult put the child in time-out when the child wants to give or get anonymous head in the park for the 613th time, but not put the child in time-out when he wants to simply be himself, to be gay? What if the child has only ever been gay in secret, among strangers with whom he has no desire to have a playdate? The child doesn't even want to know the other boys' names. He is in a hurry to get back to being an adult. What if the long-term adult self has desperately, for more than thirty-nine years, been trying to either conceal or suppress this not-so-short-term child? Hasn't the child grown up by now? What if the adult has been desperate in this way so long that this desperation has become a strangely calm anticipation? Or a kind of thrill?[1] What if the child slips up, irrevocably, and the adult tries to kill the child? A child? Really? A grandfather and father but also a child? Could it really be possible that the adult, in this one crucial, essential way, has been a child all these years?

My mother could not put my father in time-out. He was sixty-six years old. Sixty-six minutes was not long enough.

---

[1] Oscar Wilde said, "The commonest thing is delightful if only one hides it." I shared this quote with my father. He said, "There's a lot of truth to that."

Greg,

I have been so caught up in my own worries of late that I completely forgot your birthday. I am really sorry. It seems that since MomMom died, I've been really out of sorts. I have also made a few really bad choices in so-called friends. I finally decided a few days ago that I am facing the possibility of having dropped into a level of depression I haven't been in for some time. I believe that having that realization is a step in the right direction. I've made some positive changes in my behavior(s). Like quitting the bar scene and becoming more wary of people I meet. I've still got to figure out how to battle isolationism and take care of myself. But enough on me for the moment.

Happy Birthday, again. Is there anything special I can get for you that you wouldn't get for yourself? Please let me know. Also, I will go out today and at least get a real birthday card and get it in the mail.

Got to go for now.

Love you,

Dad

Assisted Living

IN THE SPRING OF 2009, TWO YEARS AFTER HE ATTEMPT-ed suicide, my father moved to Arizona. I didn't know he was considering a move. But he'd been in touch with a recruiting agent for a national rehab company located in Phoenix. They offered him a position in a 128-bed nursing home in Kingman, which is a seven hour drive down I-40 from Albuquerque. The day before he left, my father wrote me an email and broke the news. "They made me an offer worth coming out of semi-retirement for."

I didn't think it was just about the money, about the economy tanking and my father's retirement account tanking with it – though that had happened. He didn't need to move to small town Arizona, of all places, to go back to work full-time.

I called and asked him why he wasn't just going back to work full-time in Spokane. Didn't he like his job?

He said, "I don't want to see your mother in the grocery store. I saw her recently. The look she gave me –" my father's voice trailed off.

But why Kingman, Arizona? That wasn't exactly the most open and affirming place. He was a speech therapist. He could move anywhere. Why not Seattle? Or the Bay Area? I'd bet there wasn't a single gay bar within a hundred miles of Kingman. Where would he go with his guitar on Karaoke night?

"I don't really like that life," my father said. "I can't really get used it. The people that go there. They're just not the kind of people I'm used to."

What did he think, that coming out of the closet was going to be easy? Why not move some place where he at least had a fighting chance? What about the friends he'd been making lately?

My father said, "They weren't really friends." His voice had gone cold. He didn't want me to be asking these kinds of questions, but I felt strangely desperate for him. I didn't want him to give up trying.

I said, "What about that man you were sort-of seeing, the one who was divorced, who was older? The one who owns the horses and lives on a bunch of acres outside of town?"

"I don't know how to say this, son. He doesn't want any kind of commitment. He doesn't really return my calls. He only calls –" My father stopped talking.

"I'm sorry, Dad."

"It's time to move on," my father said.

My mother and father had lived together in Virginia and Nebraska, in Maryland and New Mexico, in New Jersey and Washington, but never in Arizona. There was nothing to remember in Arizona.

FOR THE FIRST several weeks in Kingman, while he looked for a new place to live, my father stayed in his popup tent trailer, in what was, truly, a typical RV park. The owner of the nursing home learned of this, and he asked my father if he wanted to stay in one of the rooms at the assisted living facility across the parking lot from the nursing home. There were a few open rooms. My father could stay for free until he found a place. My father accepted. So for about a month, he slept in a bed on wheels with electronic controls. He had a bureau with a mirror, a bathroom outfitted with safety rails, a shower with a seat, and a red call button next to the toilet. My father did not tell the other residents that he wasn't a resident. They didn't think to ask. They just assumed he was one of them.

My father did not say, "I'm just here temporarily. I work across the street. I'm waiting for my offer on a house to go through." Not once. He had breakfast and dinner with the other residents. Beef stroganoff. Chicken alfredo. Fruit medley in that syrup.

I don't know how to account for this. I don't know whether to think of it as one of the most humble things I have ever heard about anyone, or whether to see my father's reticence as a refusal to let others see how far he had fallen – and a refusal to admit this to himself, out loud, in words. Humility? Shame? Denial? Or perhaps all three at once.

My father made offers on two different houses. There was trouble, each time, with the loans – my father is no economist – but, this time, he did not steal from my mother. Both loans were denied. Each morning, after breakfast, he walked across the parking lot to work.

DURING THIS TIME, I talked with my father about once a week. He didn't tell me he was staying in an assisted living home. I didn't learn this until much later, about two years later. What he told me at the time, in an email, was this: "I've had to live in a temporary place with most of my things still packed, waiting for a permanent home."

Father's Day

MY FATHERHOOD HAS BEEN CELEBRATED NINE TIMES now, and I can't remember a single well-meant gift. No father remembers what they get for Father's Day. Not really, and this is as it should be. Father's Day gifts are supposed to be vague and generic. Something he needs but won't get for himself. When I was growing up, I gave my father soap-on-a-rope. I gave him brown socks in a three-pack. I gave him shoe polish. I gave him ties so wide they could now be worn only by supremely self-confident hipsters. He always seemed pleased with these gifts. But even as accomplished an actor as he was, he could not pretend to be thrilled. Which was okay. I was pretending, too. I pretended to have thoughtfully picked them out myself, when the truth was that my mother bought these presents for him. After I grew up and went off to college and eventually became an adult, my mother stopped giving my father gifts for Father's Day on my behalf. She didn't even send him a card. Instead, a few days before, she'd call and remind me that Father's Day was coming up, and a few days later, I would call him and we'd talk for a while on the phone.

But why did I not call my father on Father's Day in the summer of 2009? It could no longer be my mother's fault. Could I possibly have waited to email him until a few days after Father's Day because he had not gotten in touch with me, at all, for the past two years on my birthday? I wouldn't do something like that, would I?

Until now, it had never occurred to me to wonder how my father spent Father's Day when he was a boy. I wonder if that day, and the days leading up to it, were spent in fear. Or in hope and longing for the father who would be sober, kind, unpredatory. Wouldn't that have been what my father always felt for his father, on every day of his childhood – fear and longing at once?

I HAVE NEVER once feared my father. Not a single moment, not a single day. I wonder how many grown children can say such a thing.

Subject: **RE: Father's Day**

Date: Tue, 30 Jun 2009

Greg,

Really nice to hear from you. And I do understand exactly how it happens. But I have an over active imagination. I woke up yesterday morning at 5:30 sweating like a stuck pig, absolutely positive that you were trying to hide something from me. The only thing imaginable that you would hide from me was that your Mom might have cancer again. This would be something that I am incredibly vulnerable about. I still care very much and felt totally powerless. It was all I could do to get through the day … I was most grateful to hear I was wrong. You may not want to hear all about the inner me. We have discussed this in the past. I feel very deeply, but have always kept my inner self hidden, and it is obvious that I still do. It is a rare occasion for me to really open up. I was really and truly scared about the possibility that your Mom might be facing cancer again and I couldn't be there in any form for support. I told you once before that my penance for my many sins would be never to be close to Dee again. It is a forever pain that has not diminished in the past two years.

The transition from Spokane to Kingman has been interesting, but not without its problems. I've had to learn a completely new computer documentation system at work. I've made mistakes, partly because my boss never took the time to really ensure I knew what I was doing before cutting me loose. I don't believe she wants me to fail, she just didn't check up on what I was doing to make sure I was doing it right. Happy to say I haven't made any serious mistakes, just annoying ones. I really like almost all the people I work with. They are mostly friendly and helpful. The facilities I work at are all clean and well managed and I've not met a nurse who didn't know what he/she was doing. I was really depressed about the loan on the house falling through. And I've had to live in a temporary place with most of my things still packed, waiting for a permanent home. Yes, I'm lonely. But no, I'm not doing anything about it. I'm not going to try bowling yet because I go to bed around 9:30 and bowling leagues never finish that early. There is no bridge that plays at night. They only play during the day at the Senior Center. Can't do that. I have resolved, however, that when I get settled, I am going to frequent the Community Center for lunch or dinner. I don't like living like a hermit.

Like I said earlier, I don't open up often, but when I do, watch out. Right now, my fingers are tired and my shoulders ache. More later.

Love you all very much.

Dad

My Father's Memoir

I CAN'T TELL YOU MY FATHER'S STORY. THE BEST I CAN do is let him speak for himself, from time to time, so that you can at least partially come to know him, so you can see how he is both emotionally open (*It is a forever pain that has not diminished in two years*) and frustratingly vague (*I've had to live in a temporary place*) in the same email.

My father's memoir will never be written.

I can't tell you anything about what it's like to live a secret life, to be a sexually active gay man while married and in a loving relationship with a woman. When I imagine that life, it's as if I'm imagining the life of a man I've never met.

Imagine my father's memoir. Imagine the stories he might tell. Imagine how his stories would confirm or contradict, clarify or confuse the stories I am telling here. Imagine all the stories my father has not told and will never tell. How can I know him if he won't tell me his stories? How can I tell you what he won't tell me?

Transgression

THE HOUSE WAS QUIET. DEE HAD BEEN ASLEEP FOR hours, since ten or so. The boys had been asleep longer. He'd checked on them at eleven, before he got into bed himself. They'd kicked off their covers and he'd pulled them back up. It was November and the house was cold at night even with the furnace running.

He'd been in bed long enough. He hadn't slept, hadn't tried to sleep, couldn't have slept if he'd tried. He knew better. He pulled back the sheet, slid his feet to the cool wood floor, walked lightly to the closet, and took a t-shirt and jeans from two hooks at the back of the closet – he'd hung them there earlier that night – and went down the hall to the bathroom. The house was old, built in the twenties, and the worn, oak floorboards creaked with every step. No matter. He hardly noticed. His was a house of heavy sleepers. The walls creaked and the furnace knocked and whistled and the plumbing banged against the joists. He'd stopped noticing all these night sounds. He didn't hear them any more than he heard his own breathing, which was calm. Anticipation – that low electric thrum – was deeper in his chest. In the dark of the bathroom, he took off his pajamas and pulled on and zipped up his jeans. He opened the linen closet and set his pajamas on a high empty shelf. He turned and, out of habit, checked his teeth in the medicine cabinet mirror. They were fine. He'd brushed them before he'd gone to bed. For a moment, he stood tall and took his own measure. He was forty-two years old. Only a few of the hairs on his chest had gone gray. He was lean and strong. He pulled on the t-shirt, left the bathroom and went down the back stairs. In the kitchen, he took his keys off their hook. He took his wallet from the drawer and put it in his back pocket. He opened a tall cabinet door, and beside the sugar and salt and Flintstones vitamins, he found Dee's blue pill organizer. He took out her three pills for that morning, a Tuesday, and set them in a small glass bowl on the counter. He took out her penguin mug and set it beside the bowl.

Beside the door, he stepped into his boat shoes. He took his jacket from its hook. He turned the deadbolt, let himself out the side door, and walked down the rickety wooden steps to the red Ford Escort in the open carport. He turned the key in the ignition and the engine coughed and turned over. He opened the glove compartment and reached his arm behind the back panel and pulled out his cigarettes. He shook one out and put it to his lips. He wouldn't light it until he got there, until he was outside the car, waiting. He backed out of the driveway and drove off.

Self-Promotion

WALT WHITMAN IS NOT KNOWN FOR RESTRAINT OR SELF-censorship. The man wrote and published not one but several glowing, anonymous reviews of his own book.

> An American Bard at last! One of the roughs, large, proud, affectionate, eating, drinking, and breeding, his costume manly and free, his face sunburnt and bearded, his posture strong and erect, his voice bringing hope and prophecy to the generous races of young and old. We shall cease shamming and be what we really are ...
>
> No sniveler, or tea-drinking poet, no puny clawback or prude, is Walt Whitman ... The body, he teaches, is beautiful. Sex is also beautiful. Are you to be put down, he seems to ask, to that shallow level of literature and conversation that stops a man's recognizing the delicious pleasure of his sex, or a woman hers?

In the third edition of *Leaves of Grass*, Walt Whitman added an untitled poem believed to be an account of the aftermath of Whitman's love affair with a younger Irishman named George Vaughan. But Whitman cut this poem from the fourth edition and all subsequent editions of *Leaves of Grass*. It's nowhere to be found in my Modern Library copy (the "deathbed" edition). In the poem, Whitman is not his affirming, universal, celebratory self. He is abandoned and bereft.

> Sullen and suffering hours – (I am ashamed –
>   but it is useless – I am what I am;)
> Hours of my torment – I wonder if other men
>   ever have the like out of the like
>   feelings?

Is there even one other like me – distracted
– his friend, his lover, lost to him?
Is he too as I am now? Does he still rise
in the morning, dejected, thinking who
is lost to him? And at night, awaking,
think who is lost?
Does he too harbor his friendship silent and
endless? Harbor his anguish and
passion?
Does some stray reminder, or the casual
mention of a name, bring the fit back
upon him, taciturn and deprest?
Does he see himself reflected in me? In these
hours does he see the face of his hours
reflected?

My father is one other like Whitman – rising in the morning,
dejected, thinking who is lost to him. And at night, awaking,
thinking who is lost. My father harbors his friendship silent and
endless. He harbors his anguish. Stray reminders, or the casual
mention of a name, brings the fit back upon him, taciturn and
depressed. Unlike Whitman, my father has never – to my knowledge – felt this way about another man. My father feels this way –
he will always feel this way – about my mother.

THIS POEM THAT Whitman cut from the fourth edition of
Leaves of Grass was one of twelve poems that appear in Whitman's
notebooks, known to scholars as the "Live Oak, with Moss"
sequence. In these poems, Whitman is unambiguously homosexual. Whitman had written of "manly love" before, but abstractly,
celebrating human sexuality in all its forms – what one scholar
called Whitman's "cosmo-eroticism." Nowhere else in Whitman's
poetry is there such a sustained account of homosexual love.
Nowhere else in more than half a century of publishing poems is
Whitman so personal or direct. Scholars speculate that, had
Whitman published these twelve poems intact, they would have
been the first homosexual coming out account in American
literature.

Hours discouraged, Distracted,
— For he, the one I cannot
content myself without —
Soon I saw him content
himself without me,
Hours when I am forgotten —
(O weeks and months are
passing, but I believe I am
never to forget!)
Sullen and suffering hours —
(I am ashamed — but it is
useless — I am what I am;)
Hours of my torment — I
wonder if other men ever
have the like, out of the
like feelings?
Is there even one other like
me — distracted — his friend,
his lover, lost to him?
Is he too as I am now? Does
he still rise in the morning,
dejected, thinking who is lost to him?
And at night, awaking, think who is
lost?

Does he too harbor his friendship silent and endless? Harbor his anguish
and passion?
Does some stray reminder or the
casual mention of a name bring
the fit back upon him, taciturn
and deprest?
Does he see himself reflected in me?
In these hours does he see the
face of his hours reflected?

12

D. W.

But Whitman broke up the sequence, distributing them out of their chronology among the forty-five poems of the newly added "Calumus" section of the third edition (1860) of Leaves of Grass before cutting the most personal of the poems from the fourth edition (1867).

Whitman didn't just cut the poems from Leaves of Grass; he cut them from his notebooks. He took scissors and literally cut them out. One hundred years later a scholar put them back together again – humpty-dumpty style – following the order of the numbers Whitman used to title the sequence. If you look at the archive photographs of the poems you can see the joints where they've been taped back together. One hundred years later this handwritten poem sequence was made whole again.

What Walt Whitman cut from Leaves of Grass was his shame. His shame is even contained by parentheses,

> (I am ashamed –
> but it is useless – I am what I am;)

as if to acknowledge it at all is barely speakable – as if he is ashamed of his shame. Perhaps not. Perhaps he wanted nothing in his work to undermine his life-long affirmation of human sexuality in all its complexity. Or perhaps he found the poems self-pitying. I don't. I find Whitman more human, more universal without the grand first person plural, more sympathetic, because he is in so much doubt and despair, because he is, as always, seeking connection.

IN AN EMAIL he sent me less than three months after his suicide attempt, my father wrote:

I have thought many times in my life that if I could start over again, I would find a way to not be the way I am. Unfortunately, there is no way to turn the clock back and do it over. I am who I am and must find a way to live with this self and this way of life.

Acclimation

CHRISTINE, THE BOYS, AND I WENT OUT TO DINNER WITH my father on one of his visits. We went to Bumblebees, a chain Mexican restaurant within walking distance of our house, in a hip-for-Albuquerque neighborhood called Nob Hill. We sat down at a table next to six men. Three couples. They were all approximately my age, in their late thirties or early forties. They were talking and laughing. My father did not stare. He ate his burrito. He patiently listened to plot summaries of the morning's cartoons. He ranked his favorite superheroes and provided convincing justifications. He gave no sign that he was interested in the conversation at the table next to us. Three years earlier, I would have thought nothing of this. I would not have been in awe of his ability to appear as if there was nothing he longed for in that restaurant that he did not have.

When we were done with dinner, my father held the door, and we all walked out of the restaurant. When he let the door go, I looked my father in the eye. "You heard every word they said."

He nodded. "They were just talking about their lives."

I put my hand on his shoulder, and we stood there for a moment as Christine and the boys walked down the sidewalk. The cars on Central rushed by. My father and I started to follow. My father said, "I can't get used to it."

Affective Forecasting

WHEN MY MOTHER INSPECTS HER MEMORY, SHE REMEM-
bers many times when she should have wondered out loud, to
my father: Where were you? Why were you out so late? WHAT
were you doing? Really? Are you lying to me? How do I know that
what you're telling me is true? What is going on? My mother
knew risk theory. She knew that loss aversion induced a strong
bias toward the status quo. She just wasn't aware that she was
failing to apply this fundamental principle to her marriage. Or
to say that another way: in hindsight, she can see how many times
she looked the other way.

When my mother divorced my father – when she chose to
never see him again – she did not base this decision on social
science. But it turns out that this was the best thing she could
have done for both of them, according to research in the relatively
new field of affective forecasting – the study of how we predict
we will feel in the future. In one study, conducted by the psychologist Daniel Gilbert, undergraduates chose two favorite photographs from photographs they had taken all over campus, and
they developed and blew these two photos up in a darkroom
into black and white eight-by-ten glossies. Then they were told
to pick one and give Gilbert the other. They couldn't have both.

> … Now there are two conditions in this experiment. In one case,
> the students are told, 'But you know, if you want to change your
> mind, I'll always have the other one here …' The other half of the
> students are told exactly the opposite. 'Make your choice.'

… right before the swap and five days later, people who are stuck with that picture, who have no choice, who can never change their mind, like it a lot! And people who are deliberating, 'Should I return it? Have I gotten the right one? Maybe this isn't the good one? Maybe I left the good one?' – have killed themselves. They don't like their picture.

Gilbert doesn't mean the students really killed themselves. That's a figure of speech. Here's what he means. "The psychological immune system works best when we are totally stuck. When we are trapped … "

When there is no longer any possibility of a shared future. When there is nothing left but memories.

Rest Area

WE'RE DRIVING I-80, FROM our home in Lincoln, Nebraska, to northern Nevada, to visit my grandparents – my mother's parents. I am six or seven years old. Western Nebraska, northern Colorado, Utah. We stop at a rest stop. I enter the dim concrete, bunker-like men's room with my brother and my father. We all pee next to each other, the three of us in a row. I'm just tall enough to use the urinal. I don't have to go inside the stall anymore to pee.

We come back out of the building. I'm wearing my Sinclair hat, with its signature green brontosaurus logo, which my parents bought me earlier that day. The visor of my Sinclair hat helps block the bright Utah sun.

My father turns and takes a knee, so he can look my brother and me in the eyes. He says, "I don't want you to ever go into a rest area bathroom without an adult. Do you understand?" His tone is not at all harsh, but he's serious.

Why?

"I'll tell you. Bad people can be in rest area bathrooms. A man pulled a knife on me one time in a rest area bathroom. I thought he was going to kill me."

Why did he do that?

"He wanted my billfold."

Did you give it to him?

"I did."

You didn't fight?

"No. You don't fight. You never fight. He would have killed me if I did. You have to be careful. You never go into a rest area without an adult. Do you understand?"

WHEN I WAS in my twenties I drove all over the West. I drove a rusted-out, red '77 step-side Chevy truck that I'd bought from a peanut farmer in West Texas. Really. This truck had a ball mount trailer hitch, which meant, if I wanted, I could tow a horse trailer. I could haul up to 6,000 pounds. I'd ridden a horse twice in my life, three times maybe. But I liked what driving this truck with its trailer hitch said about me, about the kind of man I was. Western. Rugged. My truck – the Red Rambler – got eight miles to the gallon. This was before carbon footprints and fuel efficiency, when gas was cheap. When I drove the Red Rambler into the higher elevations, like the long climb up the mountain to Flagstaff, I was passed by sixteen-wheelers with their hazards on. I drove the shoulder, happily, without embarrassment. I drank a lot of coffee and stopped at a lot of rest areas. Every time I stopped at a rest area – or a lot of times, anyway – I thought to myself, Don't go into a rest area bathroom without an adult. I thought this even though, by some measures, I was an adult. I still think this when I stop at rest areas, my bladder full, the pressure built up in my urethra – not the pent up aching river that Whitman wrote about, but similar. Back then, it never once occurred to me – why would it? – that the man who once pulled a knife on my father might not have been a thief, might not have wanted my father's billfold, that perhaps it was my father who wanted something, or that this man wanted something that my father wouldn't give, or vice versa, or that this man with the knife had not wanted to do anything but take a leak when he turned and saw my father standing there waiting.

The Right House

WE DROVE INTO LINCOLN, NEBRASKA. UP VAN DORN, left on 27th street, and a right to 2828 Stratford Avenue. Here we were. The house where I grew up. A large gray, two-story house with light blue trim and an open front porch. It was the middle of the afternoon on a Tuesday in July. We were driving from Albuquerque to St. Paul, Minnesota, to the house where Christine grew up and where her parents still lived. This was day two of a three-day drive. It was lunchtime, a good time to stop. I hadn't been back to Lincoln since I was sixteen. Twenty-two years. At first glance, the house looked more or less the same as it looked in my memory, which I didn't expect, perhaps because of the cliché about not being able to go home again. We all got out of the car.

A dog was barking from inside the house, from the room my parents had used as an office, just to the right of the front entrance, off the living room, separated by French doors with glass doorknobs. Nobody seemed home.

The basketball hoop my father had put up for me was still there, on its post at the left hand curve of the driveway. I announced this. "The basketball hoop is still here. I remember the day my Dad poured the cement in the ground for the post. Right there." The boys were at my side. The net was old and weathered and hanging by threads from only two hooks. It may have been the same net that I had practiced on all those hours and years. It was impossible to tell.

The boys were excited for me. "I don't know how many lay-ups I shot on this basket," I said. "Probably a million."

I pointed out how my brother and I used to climb up the white fence, right there, then we pulled ourselves up to the roof of our neighbor's garage, then jumped the three feet from their garage roof to our garage roof, then climbed up to the roof of our house. Sometimes our black and white cat, Pirate, a lean tom who lived to be nineteen, would join us up there and follow us around. From the roof of our house we could look in every direction over the neighborhood.

"Granny and Grandpa let you do that?" Oliver asked, astonishment in his eyes.

"Not exactly," I said, and winked at Oliver, and then I winked at Evan, too, to be fair.

"Don't get any ideas," Christine said.

Oliver rubbed his hands together diabolically.

"The treehouse is gone," I said. "It was right there." A flower garden was in the side yard now.

"Was it like our treehouse?" Evan asked.

"Sort of."

I told them how the treehouse my father built wasn't actually connected to a tree, like ours. It was two stories, freestanding. But it felt like a treehouse because, see – and I pointed – the branches of the trees extended out and over the treehouse, so that when you stood up on the open deck of the second story there were branches and leaves all around, just like our treehouse. I told Oliver and Evan, how, as I got older, I spent less and less time in the treehouse. I kind of forgot about it, like the boy in the Shel Silverstein story *The Giving Tree*. They nodded. They knew what I meant. I would sometimes go in the treehouse as a teenager and there would be cobwebs and the smell of mildew and rot.

I sat down in the side yard of my old house where the treehouse used to be. It felt like the right thing to do. Evan climbed into my lap. I wasn't feeling the way I'd felt as we were driving into town. That heightened anticipation had gone away.

Oliver sat down beside me. I told the boys how, one day, when I was about ten, I was climbing up the ladder – which my dad had secured to the treehouse wall with only sixteen penny nails – when the nails just pulled out completely, and I fell backwards with the top rung in my hands. I fell flat on my back and the ladder fell on top of me. Right there. I pointed. I fell right onto the concrete under the basketball hoop. I was looking up through the net at the sky.

Oliver and Evan laughed. I smiled. I said it wasn't that funny. Oliver said it was probably pretty funny but I just didn't think so at the time. I said he had that exactly right.

"Did anyone see you?" Evan asked. He had a worried look on his face. I might have been hurt and no one would have been able to come to me.

"No. I must have been the only one home. I wasn't that hurt, just sort of shook up."

"Did you cry?" Evan asked.

"I probably thought that I was too old to cry," I said.

We sat together in silence for a minute or so, looking at my basketball hoop.

Oliver leaned into me. "It's okay, Dad."

"Thanks, Oliver," I said.

We got up and took a walk around the block. I narrated. I started to feel better. We turned right on Calumet Court, which was still a cobblestone street. We passed Corey Comstock's  house. He and I biked everywhere. We played CHiPs. Corey was John, I was Ponch. Our bikes would not make revving and accelerating motorcycle sounds on their own, and so we made these sounds ourselves. Corey's dad lost an arm in Vietnam and so one of his shirtsleeves was always empty, folded up neatly and pinned close to his shoulder. He smoked a cigar. I didn't mention Corey's dad. I told the boys about my paper route. I pointed out the home where I often got a dollar tip on collection days. I talked about my alarm going off so early in the mornings, how my eyelashes were sometimes glued shut. I spoke at length about the bike handling skills required to balance, at speed, a full newspaper bag over handlebars, while at the same time making an accurate throw from the street to the steps of a front porch. I spoke about making this same throw in Nebraskan winter, biking over snow and ice. This honed ability would soon be gone from the world, like a knack for Morse code or the semicolon.

We stopped at the three-cornered lot, which now had a new name and playground equipment designed for the toddler set. It had been a triangular dirt and grass lot with a backstop when I was growing up. Oliver and Evan played for a while on the structure, then swung on the swings. Christine held my hand.

We stopped by my old elementary school. The boys wanted to go inside the big brick building. Some kind of open house was going on, and parents with preschool age kids were milling around the playground, going in and out the tall front doors. I experienced the august, senatorial feeling that often came to me when I was around other parents with children even slightly younger than my children. Evan was, after all, six-years-old and soon to be in first grade. We all went inside. The high ceilings and the wooden banisters were just as I remembered them. Except that I couldn't remember ever remembering them. Perhaps it's better to say that the high ceilings and wooden banisters, and even the lemony smell of the halls, felt accurately rendered.

We walked back to the car. As we turned the corner onto Stratford Avenue, there was my old house again, the second one from the corner. I thought to myself, I love that house. I had a happy childhood here. But it wasn't as easy to access and entertain those happy memories anymore. My memories had been altered, amplified, re-interpreted. Familiar, nostalgic memories had turned darker, eclipsed by unfamiliar memories insisting on their priority, their own narrative emphasis.

I had the irrepressible feeling that something had been taken from me, or that I'd lost something, something intangible, maybe, but with the powerful emotional associations of an object, a possession, an heirloom. I kept feeling that I'd gotten something crucially wrong. My knowledge of my father's secret life had tainted and bled into the way I thought about my past. I felt that my childhood, in many of its particulars, had been somehow falsified.

The story of my childhood I had been telling myself, and others, for years, had been, it seemed to me now, a children's story. There was nothing trashy or tabloid in the vintage, age-appropriate version. No fraud. No heartbreak. No call for withering irony. No underlying narrative of bigotry and shame. All was calm and uninflamed. Not a single character disillusioned. It was hard now to make my life feel consistent, coherent, credible. I couldn't untangle and clarify all the seeming contradictions. I couldn't suppress the corrosive sense that I was an unreliable narrator of my own life.

LYDIA DAVIS, IN her essay "Remember the Van Wagenens,"
writes:

> If you don't know that this house here is Mozart's birthplace,
> you are not interested, even though you walk right past it, a great
> lover of Mozart.
>
> If you do know, you stand before it filled with a number of
> emotions and thoughts, including awe.
>
> On the other hand, if you have made a mistake, and are stand-
> ing in front of the wrong house, thinking it is Mozart's house,
> your thoughts and emotions are exactly the same as if you stood
> in front of the correct house … It won't matter unless you find
> out it was the wrong house. Then in your own eyes you will feel
> you did not really have the experience you thought you had.

I WAS STANDING in front of the right house. I still sometimes
lived here in dreams. It was true that my father, in this house
and elsewhere, had been as I had experienced him: loving, kind,
humble, with a reckless appetite for pecan pie and science
fiction. But it was also true that he was motivated on a daily basis
by the intent to deceive, so that his deception was ever-present,
whether I was aware of it or not. It was in the air I breathed.

But nothing had been lost. The past cannot be lost in the
present. Not even memories were lost, because memories are
not fixed but ever-changing, because memories do not record
the past but are only constructions invented in the present.
They are a feat of the imagination. They are made now and last
only seconds – flashes, images, evanescent, impermanent, gone.
Forever. They are not even words on a page.

As I stood and stared at the place where I grew up, a sud-
den wave of homesickness left me weak in the knees. I looked
around. It was a bright sunny day. Christine had the kids in the
car, buckled up and waiting. I caught her eye. She gave me a sad
smile, and I understood I could take as long as I wanted. But I
didn't need any more time. I walked over, got in the driver's seat,
put the car in gear, and drove off. We stopped for lunch at a
coffee shop on South Street that had not been there when I was
growing up. There was no such thing as a coffee shop in Lincoln,

Nebraska, in the seventies. Grown-ups somehow made it through their days. As we were driving out of town, I felt a migraine coming on. A silvery aura appeared in the center of my field of vision, and I knew from experience that I had about fifteen minutes before the knife blade would sink into my temple. I had to turn my head to see where I was going. I only had peripheral vision. I pulled over to the shoulder of the interstate off ramp. Christine came around to drive, and I went around to the passenger seat.

Migraines paid me a visit five or six times a year, always at the release of some tension. After something I'd been worried about for a long time had come to an end, the silvery aura reliably presented itself. A few different times I'd gotten a prescription for migraine medication, but I'd never filled it. There was something I savored about settling into durable, predictable, and thought-numbing pain. A good migraine meant that I could stop tormenting myself with my own thoughts and imagination and endless speculation, my own smoldering judgment and confusion. My migraine was like a three-hour existential hall pass from the interminable class that was myself.

Remembering Remembering

SOMETIMES EVAN SAYS, "REMEMBER WHEN WE VISITED your old house, Dad? Remember when we walked around the block and you showed us where your friends lived and that park where you played? Remember that place on the walk to your school where you jumped from one wall to the other? Remember when we walked around in your old school and the lady came out and you said, 'I used to go to school here.'? Remember that?"

Now I can't remember my old neighborhood without remembering my children walking with me through my old neighborhood, holding my hand or with their arms swinging at their sides. I can't remember my old neighborhood without remembering Evan remembering my neighborhood.

VLADIMIR NABOKOV, IN *Speak, Memory: an Autobiography Revisited*, writes,

I confess I do not believe in time. I like to fold my magic carpet after use, in such a way as to superimpose one part of the pattern upon another. Let visitors trip. And the highest enjoyment of timelessness – in a landscape selected at random – is when I stand among rare butterflies...

Mysteries

I'M REMEMBERING MY MOTHER AND father sitting in the living room of my childhood home. They're reading in their separate chairs. I am nine years old.

My mom is reading a Dick Francis horse-racing mystery. She has already read, several times, all twenty of Dick Francis's horse-racing mysteries published up to that point, 1980. She buys them in hardcover, right when they're published.

Re-reading these mysteries does not require any willful forgetting on my mother's part. No denial whatsoever. She can never remember who did what to whom. It's a mystery every time. She loves this about her memory. It has ceased to astonish her. She gets to re-read the books she loves over and over. It takes about a year before she can confidently re-read a book with the satisfactory amount of amnesia, so that the book is pleasantly familiar, but surprising. My father is reading a science fiction novel. He is far away, on a cold planet in a remote solar system, a mining colony, an outpost in galactic Siberia. My parents' appetite for reading is sensual; like a pheromone it fills the house. Has a day ever passed in our home when I do not see them reading? I can't remember. I don't think so. Our house is so often this quiet and calm; we are all reading, somewhere, if not together in this room. It is summer, evening, bedtime a long way off. The hour of lamps.

There is nothing I want to do more than read in this quiet living room with my mother and father. Nothing is calling me away. I am happy. I am reading a Hardy Boys mystery on the brown shag carpet. I'm just out of my parents' sight, in that narrow four foot space on the other side of the green sofa, beside the dark, walnut built-in bookshelf that runs the length of the room. My brother Chris and I own all fifty-eight books of the original Hardy Boys mysteries – all the blue hardbacks, every single one – organized by number along the bottom of the bookshelf. The desire to read is my oldest, strongest desire. Chris could read very early, at three or four. He is a year and a half older, and he loves reading as much as my parents. He is always reading. In the room we share, our twin beds are against opposite walls, and now I am remembering staring at my brother in the dark. Chris is reading a Hardy Boys mystery by the light of the streetlamp through our open-curtained windows. I cannot read yet because in this memory I am five, but I have a Hardy Boys mystery in bed with me anyway. I am studying the pictures for clues, pretending to read, claiming to read. I am burning with impatience and desire. I remember. I want so badly for the words to announce themselves. But soon I am nine and I am Joe Hardy, the younger brother, and I am on the case. My father, the detective Fenton Hardy, has disappeared yet again, and Frank and I must find him, and solve the mystery.

 I am remembering now how happy I was then, that calm, quiet happiness, so still and focused, a happiness outside of time, a happiness I so often see in Oliver, who is always reading, every single day, morning, afternoon, evening. Now he's reading the Usagi Yojimbo series, graphic novels by Stan Sakai, about the adventures of a samurai rabbit.

SEVENTEEN BOOKS FROM this series are stacked right now in two neat piles on our coffee table in the living room. Oliver has read them all and started over. We need to go to the library for more.

Oliver Cooney-Martin: *Untitled*, 2009

Master of None

MY FATHER WAS A SEVENTH-GRADE P.E TEACHER. HE drove all over the Midwest selling pharmaceuticals for Squibb. He sold real estate for Century 21. He sold gasohol, an alternative gasoline and alcohol fuel mixture, for the National Gasohol Commission. He weatherized houses. He worked in a hardware store, in the nuts and bolts area; he was promoted to kitchen design. He went back to school in his fifties, earning an under- graduate and master's degree in speech pathology. He learned sign language and worked at a school for the deaf. He took a job in a nursing home helping elderly men and women who had suffered strokes regain the ability to speak. After harrowing, life- altering setbacks, patients looked to my father to help them recover their voice.

In other words, after more than thirty years of catch-as- catch-can employment, my father found his calling. I have never seen my father at work with his patients, but it's easy for me to imagine him: patient, kind, gentle, encouraging.

Everywhere my family moved, because of my mother's career in academics, in government, and finally in administration at three universities in three different states, my father found a new job. Each move left him out of work, sometimes for months at a time. If he was discouraged, disheartened, depressed, I did not know it. When I was in middle school and high school, I was often embarrassed by him, by his presence, his availability. I felt the need to explain why, always, my father picked me up from school, drove me to and from practice in his old white Chrysler Newport. When I think of my embarrassment now, I wince with shame. I have to remind myself that there was no such thing then as stay-at-home dads. It was a different time.

I can still remember coming out the front doors of middle school and seeing the big white Chrysler parked alongside the curb, my father behind the wheel reading a paperback. More than once, I kept my eyes straight ahead and walked right past him. I walked the two miles home. He pulled into the driveway fifteen or twenty minutes later and came in the house wondering what had happened. I said that I hadn't seen him. He did not challenge my lie.

MY LOVE FOR my mother was then, and still is, unambivalent. We spend time together easily. When I was growing up, I liked to go grocery shopping with her, just for her company. We watched old movies together on weekends, Westerns and Mysteries, especially. For my encyclopedic knowledge of Alfred Hitchcock and Cary Grant, of Katherine Hepburn and Paul Newman, I have my mother to thank. My mother loved, and still loves, college football and basketball. We attended games together on campus. We watched games together on television, shouted the same encouragement and advice at the coaches on the screen. We played, and still play, pinochle and cribbage with an intensity that Christine finds unsettling. My mother told me that I could do whatever I set my mind to do. She taught me to work hard, to pick myself up and dust myself off when I failed, and try again. She instilled in me a lifelong belief in myself. But it's also true that my mother worked hours as hard and long as the fathers of most of my friends growing up. Harder. Longer. As a woman professional in the 1970s and 80s in the all-male field of economics, she had to be better than, not just as good as, the men she worked with, taught with, published alongside.

WHEN MY FATHER was a teenager, he drove his father around from bar to bar on Saturdays. They started around nine in the morning. They kept going until my father's father was too drunk to walk. All day, my father would wait in the car, parked outside on the curb, and read a paperback. Late in the afternoon or in early evening, he'd deliver his father safely home, stinking drunk. Then he'd have the car that night to go out with his friends or out on a date with a girl.

MY FATHER DID not play sports well. He'd been cut from his high school football team. But he threw countless balls to me and caught countless balls in return. He rebounded countless shots. My father took me to cub scout meetings, to webelos and boy scout meetings. He had been an Explorer Scout himself and so was undaunted by the task of whittling a car from a wooden block and then painting and racing it, with its lead weights, down a varnished ramp. He took me camping. He took me out into the woods along the Platte River to cut wood for our fireplace for winter. Each November, I helped him make candles for Christmas presents, pouring the hot, colored wax into molds, in his shop in the basement. He'd never taken a lesson, but he taught me to play the piano and the guitar.

When we spent time together, never once did there seem to be something else he would rather be doing. Even the thought of such a possibility occurs to me only now.

On the coldest of dark winter mornings, when it was too cold to bike, we sat in the warmth of the Chrysler and folded and rubber-banded newspaper after newspaper, and then he drove me house to house delivering them through the neighborhood. I didn't have to ask. My alarm would go off, and he'd already be awake, downstairs at the breakfast table, drinking coffee, waiting, the car warming up in the driveway.

My father never wanted more from me than I could give. He never found my effort insufficient. I did not need to try harder, give more, or be any way other than I already was. He was proud of me. He told me so all the time.

But I was not proud of him, not then. I was not grateful for his time, and I did not consider his sacrifice, on my mother's behalf, admirable or important. I wished that he could be more like the fathers of other boys I knew – with their suits and tasseled shoes, their understated assuredness. The fathers of these boys were not out of work. They were not like my father; I could not even imagine them being like him. My father was not timid. He shook hands firmly; he looked people in the eye. But he was entirely unassuming. Humble. He radiated humility. He still does. But I was afflicted with striving, ambition, a longing to become "known," and so I considered my father's humility a flaw, not the rare virtue that it was. I did not consider my father ahead of his time in his unresentful willingness to support and encourage my mother as she became the first tenured female professor of Economics at the University of Nebraska, and then the first and only female full professor in the University of Nebraska's College of Business Administration, as she took a job in the White House, and then with Congress, as she became one of only a handful of female Business School Deans in the country. I did not see my father as a fully complex character in his own right in our nation's slow but inexorable pursuit of equality.

My father was always there, but I did not really see him. Or if I did, he was slightly out of focus – either because of my own adolescent embarrassment or because of his own calculations entirely unknown to me. I thought for many years as an adult that my failure to acknowledge him, to know and cherish him the way I cherished my mother, was my failure only.

My Father's Fiction

FOR TWO YEARS DURING MY CHILDHOOD, WHEN I WAS nine and ten, my father did not hold a job but instead stayed home and wrote. He wrote science fiction. He studied craft. He went to a weeklong summer writer's conference, where his teacher was the science fiction novelist Frank Herbert, who wrote the *Dune* series. My father met other writers at the conference and corresponded with them. He wrote daily, according to a schedule he set out for himself and followed. He did this while I was in elementary school, just as I am now writing, at this very moment, while Oliver and Evan are in elementary school. My father wrote in the office of our home on Stratford Avenue, in the room where that dog was barking behind the blinds on that July afternoon when Oliver, Evan, Christine, and I visited the house on our way to St. Paul. My father was disciplined. He completed a first draft of a novel. It was never published. He wrote short stories and sent them off to magazines. They were never published. I remember the rejection letters coming in the mail.

My father never showed anything he wrote to my mother.

The drafts of those stories and that novel no longer exist, and so there's no going back now and looking through them for clues, to try and piece together the themes and preoccupations my father returned to again and again. There's no way now to see how he attempted to enact his confusion and alienation, his shame and duplicity, his humility, his humor, his wonder, his love and his sense of being loved and unloved.

I am unsentimental about "things" to a fault. I can fit all the possessions I treasure in a backpack. I don't keep books I don't like, even if I bought them in hardcover. There's no single object, no thing, I can't do without. I am always trying to find a way to throw things away while Christine is at work. I bury knickknacks and crap of all kinds in the bottom of the garbage and hope not to get caught. The emptier our house is the more I feel at home. I would make a good monk. I like the way light spills through open windows into empty rooms. I would sleep on a sleeping bag on the floor without complaint. More than once, I've suggested seriously to Christine that we sell our home and live in a yurt, off the grid, deep in the wilderness. I've been told by people I trust that this particular aspect of my personality is pathological.

But I wish I could have those manuscripts, those drafts of my father's stories he wrote when I was a boy, during that time when he was the age I am now, the time when it was irrevocably dawning on him that he was not who he was pretending to be, that he had been in denial a long time, but that denial was no longer working. That time when so much of his life was good and happy and so much of his life was deception – and he knew it and kept going. What words, what sentences, did he put down then? What was the balance between action and reflection? Were the conflicts rooted in situations – a star likely to explode, a huge asteroid on a deadly trajectory, approaching the colony at terrible speed? Or were there more internal conflicts the characters faced, for which they had no good answers? What shape did these stories take? How did these conflicts play out? How did these stories end?

I'm aware that in a good story a character has to want something badly, and this character cannot get what he wants. Not really. He gets something else. Knowing this doesn't make the loss of my father's stories, thousands and thousands of words, any easier.

Suicide is Painless

WHEN I WAS NINE YEARS OLD, I RECEIVED MY FIRST rejection letter from Random House. I'd sent them a deeply affecting and darkly comic novel about a group of farm animals, far from home, working in an army hospital. The book was called M*U*S*H.

I'd been determined to send my novel out, and my elementary school librarian had helped me look up the publisher's address in New York and helped me draft the proposal letter itself. I remember her well. She was tall and thin, with dark, curly hair. She was older than my mother but younger than my grandmother. She was always suggesting new books for me to read. I remember showing her the rejection letter – the first letter I'd ever received on letterhead. The letterhead was red. I was trying my best to contain my disappointment, when she did something I will always remember, something I did not know was possible. She told me that the Sheridan Elementary School Library would publish my book. She helped me laminate the covers and bind the thin, wide-ruled gray paper with gold clasps. We glued a tan folder in the back, and on three-by-five blank stock paper, we typed up author and title and subject cards for the card catalog. We set my book on a small easel on a low shelf near the entrance to the library. Each day, I checked to see if my book was still on display, and one day it wasn't. Someone had checked out my book. For a long time after that, I checked the card in the back of the book to see the names of the kids who were reading my book, the way one might now check their book's Amazon.com ranking.

In publishing my book, my librarian was saying: I see you. I see how much time you spend here. You love to read, you love to write, you love books, you want to be a writer. Be a writer. I have never forgotten. What a gift, the gift of recognition. The gift of permission. Be who you are. It means everything, and when others who matter give it to you, it becomes easier, though never easy, to give that permission to yourself.

 M*U*S*H WASN'T REALLY autobiographical, unless you count that once a week I sat on the couch beside my father and we religiously watched the television show *M*A*S*H*. We popped popcorn and arrived in the basement a few minutes early bristling with heightened anticipation. We sat raptly as the helicopter appeared on the screen, and we listened to the instrumental version of the show's theme song, "Suicide is Painless." I learned to play this song on the piano, sight-reading from my *American Movie Hits for Beginners* songbook. Before my voice changed, I sang along also, hitting all the high notes. *And I can take or leave it if I please.*

My father and I watched this show together for years. We laughed when Corporal (and later Sergeant) Maxwell Klinger dressed in drag but could not, could never, get his section 8. Maybe I understood, on some unconscious level, how much this hit close to home. Maybe my father studied me when I laughed. Maybe he said, "You know why that's so funny, don't you?" But I don't think so. I don't know if he identified with Klinger at all.

We watched as commanding officer and beloved, happy-go-lucky Colonel Henry Blake learned that he was going home in the final episode of season three. We watched him say his good-byes. At the end of the episode, we learned that Henry's plane had been shot down over the ocean and he'd died. Maybe we cried. Maybe we could hardly bear our sadness for Radar, the incredibly competent company clerk and bugler, because Henry Blake had been like the father Radar never had.

We could not understand what Margaret "Hot Lips" Houlihan saw in Frank Burns, but we appreciated the dramatic irony of their righteous piety set against Burns cheating on his wife. We watched when Hawkeye learned that his best friend, the cut-up Captain "Trapper" John McIntyre, had been discharged while Hawkeye was on R&R in Tokyo. Trapper did not leave a note. He gave Radar a kiss on the cheek to pass on to Hawkeye. We didn't know that the nickname "Trapper" referred to his being caught having sex in a bathroom on a train.

Maybe we laughed along with the laugh track during the episode where Hawkeye keeps asking what the initials in B.J.'s name really stand for, and B.J. keeps saying, "Anything you want." Maybe I laughed – I probably did – but I could not have understood why.

In the scenes set in the E.R., there was never a laugh track. The series creators hadn't wanted a laugh track at all. Now, on DVD, you have the option to watch the show without a laugh track, so if you don't feel like laughing, there's no laughter – yours or anyone else's.

For years, my father and I watched Captain Hawkeye Pierce's biting, quick wit, his deepening empathy, his dedication to his patients and to the show in which he was the star. Had we ever met a man so willing to grant us access to his emotional life? We watched as his simmering, erotic, antagonistic relationship with Margaret faded and their friendship matured and became beautiful. It's hard for me to watch Alan Alda grow old, to watch him play other, less  sympathetic characters in Woody Allen movies. I can't even watch him as himself on *Scientific American Frontiers*, on PBS, as he takes us from the depths of the conscious mind to the outer reaches of the universe.

My father and I watched the show's finale, on February 28, 1983, along with the rest of America. It was then the most watched television show in American history, with 106 million viewers. The show was two and a half hours long. I'd just turned twelve years old.

The Korean War is ending, and as the show begins we discover that Hawkeye Pierce has been sent to a mental hospital where he is being treated by Dr. Sidney Freedman, a gentle psychiatrist with a bushy mustache. Hawkeye has repressed some memories of a particular bus trip, and Freedman is helping him get them back. There was a soldier on the bus, and Hawkeye passed him a bottle of whiskey. No. The soldier was wounded and needed plasma. The bus stopped to pick up villagers and more wounded soldiers. There was an enemy patrol in the area. The bus pulled over. Everyone needed to stay quiet. One village woman had a live chicken that would not stop squawking. Hawkeye snapped at her. "Keep that damn chicken quiet!" The woman quieted the chicken. No. The chicken was a baby and the mother smothered her baby and now Hawkeye is sobbing.

I had never before seen a grown man weep, much less weep so fully, so openly, uninhibited, completely without restraint. Hawkeye Pierce was wild with grief and remorse. I can't remember if I was weeping, too, or if my father was weeping. That's not something I can consciously recall. I had no idea then about the burden of memory and its costs and consequences. That was something I would still have to learn.

Oliver Cooney-Martin: *Untitled*, 2009

Fairies

OLIVER LOST ANOTHER TOOTH–HIS SEVENTH OR EIGHTH. We'd lost count. He put it under his pillow at bedtime in his wrinkled and worn tooth fairy envelope. The next morning, Christine and I were in the kitchen drinking coffee and making lunches for school, when we heard the boys' bedroom door open. Oliver usually woke up about half an hour before Evan. Christine looked at me, her face panicked. "Did you put a dollar in the tooth fairy envelope?"

"That's not my department," I said.

Christine glared at me, wishing that this was somehow not as true as it was.

We went out to the living room. Oliver was sitting in the middle of the couch in his pajamas, his unhappy face still warm and red from sleep. The envelope was in his lap.

"Good morning, honey," Christine said and sat next to Oliver. I sat on the other side of him.

"You forgot," Oliver said.

Christine hesitated. Then she said, "I'm sorry, Oliver."

"I know there's no tooth fairy, Mom. I'm eight years old. No Santa Claus, either."

"No unicorns," I added.

Oliver smiled, though he didn't want to.

"Oh, Oliver," Christine said. She kissed his cheek. Oliver didn't rub this off with the back of his hand.

"Don't worry," Oliver said. "I won't tell Evan."

"Please don't," Christine said. "He's little."

"Do I still get my dollar?" Oliver asked.

"You actually get two dollars," I said. "There's a one dollar fine when the tooth fairy forgets, and a sweet, innocent child has to figure out the hard truths of life all on his own."

"When Mommy forgets," Oliver corrected. "Two dollars, Mom?"

"Of course, Oliver," Christine said forlornly.

"Mommy will forgive herself sometime next week," I said.

"It's okay, Mom."

"Oliver," I said. "I should probably tell you something else."

"What?"

"You know how Easter is this Sunday."

Oliver nodded.

"There's no Easter bunny, either."

"Gregory!"

Oliver erupted in a fit of giggling. His eyes were wide.

"It's hard, I know. But it's true. Rabbits don't have much to do with eggs. You just don't see it in nature. Chickens and rabbits are hardly ever friends."

"You can't tell your brother that," Christine said.

"You'll still get your chocolate," I said.

Oliver's giggling was making it hard for him to catch his breath.

"And Oliver," I said, "you know that old man, Karl, who walks around the block every morning, right when we're on our way to school, the old man with the cane. You know, Karl?"

"Yeah."

"He's not real, either."

Oliver wheezed for breath. There were tears in his eyes.

"Life just sometimes isn't the way it seems. Karl is just a figment of your imagination."

Oliver shouted, "Dad!"

I had bailed Christine out yet again. I was feeling pretty good about the way things were going. "I'm really sorry, Oliver. Growing up is hard."

"Dad!" Oliver shouted again.

"What?"

"You have to stop. I peed my pants."

"Really?"

"Yes!"

"You're too old to pee your pants," I said.

"It's okay. Go to the bathroom," Christine said. "And then you have to take a bath."

Oliver went into the bathroom. Christine went to pick out his clothes for school.

SO THIS SWEET, good moment – the tooth fairy story – happened, and not five minutes later, while Oliver was taking a bath and while Evan was still sound asleep, I thought of my father and his suicide attempt and his molestation and his secret life. *Life just isn't the way it seems.* My mood turned black. I thought, "Does *everything* have to be about that?" I was tired of thinking about my father. And I was tired of remembering, at innocent and ordinary moments, that I'd failed to explain to my children why their grandparents had divorced.

Two years had passed, and still I had not told the boys anything. I had not told them that their grandfather was gay. I wanted to. I wanted them to know. It seemed like every month a new state was taking up the issue of gay marriage, and it seemed like every month another teenager killed himself because he was being mocked or threatened or bullied for being gay, and I wanted my sons to know that I considered this the most

 important moral issue we faced as a country since Rosa Parks and Martin Luther King, that this was not just important, generally, but that it was important to me, to their aunt Molly and her partner Anne, who was not yet officially Aunt Anne. It was important to their grandfather, even if he wouldn't talk about it.

THERE WERE ODD times when I had the impulse to just blurt it out to one of the boys. Your grandparents divorced because your grandfather is gay. That's why. That's the reason. I wanted you to know that.

I'd say goodbye to my father and hang up the phone and see that Oliver was studying me, as if he could search my face for the clues he needed to puzzle the mystery out all on his own.

Object Lesson

WHEN I WAS NINE OR TEN YEARS OLD, I WAS DOING MY chores one Saturday morning, vacuuming the upstairs, the main floor, the basement, an hour or so of work I barely resented because that's just the way it was. Growing up, I had chores every Saturday morning before I could go out and play. I helped set and clear the table every night as well. Old school. My parents did not subscribe to the customer service model of parenting, relentlessly polling their children's comfort and satisfaction. I was not an indentured servant, and there was nothing to plow, but I was expected to do my share and I did.

I was changing out the carpet tool, the most common attachment, the long one with the foot lever and rotating brush-bar and stiff bristles. I was about to replace it with the small crevice tool, for hard to reach tight places and dusty corners, when my father appeared.

He said, "I want to show you something."

I nodded.

He picked up the vacuum's main handle and began finger-ing the little metal button near its open end, pushing it up and down, so that it recessed and then popped up, recessed and then popped up.

"See that," my father said.

"Okay," I said.

"That's the penis."

My father didn't stop to see if this struck me as unusual.

He then grasped the carpet attachment and held it low and still for me, as if it might wriggle away before we had the chance to examine it.

"See this." He pointed to the hole in the metal, the hole in which the small metal button fitted so nicely and securely. You might think I could see what was coming next, but I could not. My father said, of the hole, "This is the vagina." He looked at me.

I'd never had the word "vagina" before spoken to me directly. It wasn't a word that came easily to my ears. I was in fourth or fifth grade. I felt dizzy and hot. My father said, "Here's how it works." Then he showed me how the main handle slid inside the carpet attachment for a few inches and then how the round metal button popped up inside the hole. My father looked up, satisfied. The basic assemblage of the vacuum was something I understood. Here was an act I was deeply familiar with, an act I had performed without self-consciousness each and every Saturday, for at least two years – we are talking about countless, deft and skilled iterations, in all sorts of rooms and contexts. I took pride in my vacuuming.

"See," he said. He pressed the metal button with his thumb, pulled the carpet attachment out, and returned to me the main handle. I took it reluctantly. He handed me the carpet attachment, as well, even though I was done with it, for now.

"Go ahead," he said. My father waited. It was my turn. He was patient. I inserted the carpet attachment into the main handle until the button popped up into the hole.

I looked at my father.

"That's it," he said. "Just like that."

My father put his hand on my shoulder. "Okay, son," he said, and left the room.

This was the sex talk my father had with me. A few weeks or months later, he handed me a book to read, and I did read it, extensively, and I studied its pencil sketch illustrations, but we never talked about it, not even once. When I was done with the book – when the anxiety of having the book and its contents in my room outweighed my curiosity – I put it on the mantel of the fireplace in the basement. For days it rested there calmly. Then it was gone.

I WISH THE vacuum cleaner story was less strange and more apocryphal. A funny family anecdote – the kind every family has. For more than thirty years, when I'm in the presence of vacuuming, when I hear that unmistakable sound of suction, the words *penis* and *vagina* come to me, unbidden. My father's anatomy lesson has stayed with me, charged with surreal significance, waiting for me to puzzle it out. He was entirely sincere – he was neither mocking me nor the act of vacuuming. My father was not given to weird or creepy explanations of ordinary phenomena. He was trying to tell me something important. But the penis does not go into the vagina like that, sliding into one bigger hole and then popping up out of another, smaller hole. And the round metal part that goes up and down is never called a penis. It's sometimes called a "button-lock" and sometimes called a "nipple." My father had it all wrong.

The Romantic Sperm

I CAME HOME FROM WORK, AND OLIVER WAS SITTING on the couch. He wasn't reading. He was just sitting there. He looked stunned.

He said, "Dad, you won't believe what happened."

"Try me."

"Mom read me that book."

It took me a few seconds to make the connection. "Really? That book? The *WHERE DID I COME FROM?* book?"

"Yes!"

"Mom didn't tell me she was going to read you that book today. I thought I was going to have to read you that book."

"She didn't tell me EITHER!" Oliver shouted. He wasn't really upset. Just a little shaken up. He was enjoying himself, the two of us acting our parts, saying our lines. "Mommy sat down right next to me. She had the book and just started reading it." He was shaking his head, in part lingering disbelief, part mock disbelief.

"How did you handle it?"

"I screamed."

Christine came into the living room from the kitchen. She had a huge grin on her face. "He ran around the house. He hid in the closet. He kept shouting, 'Are you trying to kill me? Why are you doing this to me?' He was like a character in a Hilda Raz cartoon."

Oliver's cheeks burned red, but his eyes were shining and his smile was so big I could see his missing teeth.

"We laughed a lot," Christine said. "I told him, 'Mama Kay read this exact same book to me when I was nine, and I thought I was going to die. Now, I have to read it to you. It's part of my job.'"

"I thought I was going to have a heart attack," Oliver said.

"Where's Evan?"

"He's at Sam's," Christine said.

"Mommy planned the whole thing," I said.

"I know," Oliver said.

"It was an ambush," Christine said. "I'd been putting it off and putting it off and I just decided today that I couldn't wait any longer. You're not mad at me."

"Hardly," I said. "Maybe Oliver is, though. Oliver?"

Oliver growled.

Christine went back into the kitchen.

I sat down next to Oliver. "Wow. Big day. That's a lot to take in. Have you had a snack? Can I get you a glass of water?"

"I'm okay."

"It's a pretty funny book," I said. "It really spells it all out."

"You can say that again," Oliver said.

"The romantic sperm," I said, quoting the book.

"Dad, stop."

"Any questions?" I asked.

"No!"

"Okay," I said. "Anytime. If you want to ask me about it, you can. I'm here for you."

He nodded.

"Where's the book?"

"I made Mommy put it away."

I went into the kitchen. Christine was making spaghetti with Trader Joe's flame broiled turkey meatballs, which were always a big hit. "That was easy enough," I said.

Christine slapped my shoulder. "It was a blast. We cracked up. I had to revise the book some as I went along. It's great, but it's a little out of date. I told him that sex isn't just about making babies. That people have sex just to express their love for one another. I told him that the man doesn't have to get on top of the woman. The woman can get on top of the man. There were all sorts of ways to get the job done. He looked at me with these really big eyes. Then he screamed."

October 12, 2009

Dear Oliver,

While I was visiting the Hoover Dam a couple of weeks ago, I was thinking it would have been more fun if you could have been there, too. So I bought this license plate for you. Sorry they didn't have one with "Oliver" on it, but I hope your last name works just as well.

I hope you are doing well in school and having a good time in all your other activities.

Love,

Grandpa

October 12, 2009

Dear Evan,

I was visiting the Hoover Dam a couple of weeks ago and thought about how you might have enjoyed seeing it too. So I got this little license plate with your name on it for you.

I hope you are enjoying school and having a fun time in all your activities.

I love you,

Grandpa

My Mother's Father-in-Law

MY MOTHER WAS VISITING, AND I TOOK HER OUT TO breakfast after we dropped off the boys at school. We sat down with our coffee and tea. I said, "Did you ever meet Dad's father?" I'd never asked her this question before. I had never thought to ask. I just assumed that because I hadn't ever met him, and because she had never told me otherwise, that she hadn't met him either.

She said, "I did. I met him once."

"Tell me," I said.

My mother nodded. She took a sip of tea – a pause for effect, like a veteran author at a packed auditorium reading. My mother is a born storyteller. "It was the day before Thanksgiving, 1969," she said. "We were visiting your aunt Edna, in Springfield. We'd been married for three years. Chris was six months old. Sometime in the afternoon, Edna left to run an errand.

"When she came back an hour or so later, she came into the living room where we were sitting and talking with your uncle Dennis. I don't know where your cousins were, probably running around the neighborhood somewhere. Edna said, 'Guess who turned up at the bus station.'"

My mother interrupted herself and said, "I'm not going to do their southern accents."

I thanked her.

She went on. "So there he was. Jake Martin was dressed in work slacks and a long-sleeved button down shirt. He was clean-shaven. He was a small man, several inches shorter than your father. His hair was thin and waxed back slick against his head. I noticed right away that he was sober. He said in a quiet voice, 'Edna bought me a ticket so I decided to come.'

"Jake said hello to Dennis who met his eye and nodded his head but did not stand up to shake his hand. Then Jake said to your father, 'Hello, son.'

"Your father would not look up, would not respond. He was scowling and shaking his head.

"The whole room went cold. It was quiet for a long time, the kind of quiet no one wants to fill or break. You know the kind.

"I could see that your father was not going to introduce me, which was very unlike him. He was always the soul of politeness.

"Jake took a few steps into the room towards me and said, 'I'm Jake Martin. It's a real pleasure to meet you.'

"I shook his hand and said it was good to meet him, too.

"Chris was sleeping in my lap, and Jake bent over a little and looked at him. He said, 'You have a beautiful boy.'

"I said, 'Thank you. We finally decided to keep him.' And that made Jake Martin smile a little, and nod his head, and I felt that was a small, good thing I could do in that moment, though I don't think your father appreciated it.

"I didn't know exactly when the last time your father had talked to his father, but it had been at least ten years. He'd told me more than once that he never wanted to see his father again. He wanted him out of his life completely.

"I knew that Jake Martin had been an awful drunk and had beaten your MomMom and Edna and Lilian. But that was all I knew.

"It was the middle of the afternoon. There wasn't much to talk about. That was the most frustrating thing about spending time with anyone in your father's family. They didn't talk politics. They didn't follow sports. If ever there was a time to talk about football, this was the time. I don't know what we talked about. Every minute felt like an hour.

"Your father sat looking at his hands. It was like he'd been turned to stone.

"Jake could read the situation. He knew he wasn't wanted there, except by Edna, who wanted so desperately to hold on to the idea of them all being a family. She always wanted that. She had a family of her own, three kids around the age Oliver and Evan are now, and she was still trying to find some way to reconcile her father with everyone.

"Edna said things like, 'Isn't it wonderful we're all together? Isn't it wonderful Dad could come?'

"No one answered. Your brother woke up and started screaming, which at least gave us something to talk about. I gave him a bottle. But I didn't leave and take him into the next room. I didn't want to leave your father. And eventually Chris quieted down.

"Edna had made reservations at the officers' club for dinner. She'd hired a babysitter for Chris and your cousins. She had the whole thing planned out.

"Now let me just say this here, before I say anything else. I know plenty of stories about how awful Jake Martin was when your father was growing up. But I don't care. Jake Martin should not have been put in the situation they all put him in that night.

"When your father was five or six, Jake Martin broke into their house and he took scissors and he pulled every article of clothing MomMom had out of her drawers – underwear, bras, shirts, pants, shorts, socks – and he cut each one of them up into tiny pieces. He did this in the middle of the day, while your father and his sisters were at school and while MomMom was at work. It must have taken him hours. He scattered the pieces on the bed. Your MomMom was hanging on by her fingernails and now the only clothes she had were the clothes she wore on her back.

"And that's not the saddest thing. Not by half. Here's the

saddest thing: MomMom told me once that she would have let
Jake beat her every day of her life – that's how much she loved
him – but she couldn't let him beat the children. What does that
say about how much your MomMom thought she was worth?
What does a child learn who witnesses that?

"So we go to the officer's club. Your father still hasn't said a
word, not to me, not to anyone. I don't remember much about
that night, but I remember I was in awe of your father's silence.

"Everybody got dressed up, but Jake is in the clothes he
came in. That thin long sleeve shirt and polyester slacks. I don't
know that he even brought a suitcase. So we're sitting there
at the table at the club. Dennis orders a round of drinks. Then he
orders another round. And it takes a while for the food to come
and so everybody's getting pretty loose. So then your father
decides to talk and he orders a round of drinks. Goddam it. Why?
Because he doesn't want to be shown up by his brother-in-law?
I don't think so. Your father wasn't like that. He didn't compete.
No. It was because his father was sitting there at the table with
us. What I think now, all these years later, is that he wanted to see
his father fall apart in front of me. I remember exactly what I
was thinking as I watched Jake Martin drink his first drink and
then his second and then his third. I thought, 'I wouldn't do this
to a dog.' It felt more and more like a set-up. Were these people
stupid? Didn't they know what was going to happen?

"So Jake gets more talkative. There are beads of sweat on
his forehead, and he's mopping at his face with his cloth napkin.
He starts slurring his words. His eyes are shining. At some
point he says, 'I was a good father. Let me tell you that. I can say
that can't I?'

"No one answers.

"'Edna, I can say that, can't I?' Jake says, more desperately
this time. 'I was a good father.'

"Edna says, 'You tried. I believe that.'

"Your father turns to Edna then. He's burning holes into her
with his eyes.

"Edna blurts out to the whole room, 'He tried. Sometimes he didn't try hard enough.'

"Jake Martin nods. He narrows his eyes and turns to your father. He says, 'Okay, then. Was I a good father? What do you say, son?'

"I'll never forget that. That ruthlessness. Your father stared at his father. He stared at his father for a long time. He didn't say anything. They stared at each other. It was awful. It was awful at the time, and it's even more awful now, knowing what I didn't know then.

"I don't know what happened next. I don't know when we left or what else was said.

"That night, your father sat up for hours, shaking with anger. He sat at the end of the bed. He never changed out of his clothes. I woke up in the middle of the night and he was gone. I talked about this one time with your MomMom, about how some nights your father never went to sleep at all, about how I'd wake up and not know where he was. She told me that he used to do that all the time as a little boy. They called him 'the night wanderer.' MomMom would wake up for some reason, maybe she heard something, and your father wouldn't be in his bed. She'd look and look and then she'd find him – six, seven, eight years old – sitting out on the front porch in the dark.

"The next morning Jake Martin was gone. Edna took him and put him back on the bus to North Carolina.

"I can see the officer's club right now. I can see us at that table. Jake didn't get loud. You know how it is with some drunks. But not Jake. I remember. It was almost as if he was drunk after the first drink. Once he started, it didn't take much. They should not have done that to him.

"I never saw Jake Martin again. Your father never saw him again, either."

Survival Rate

ACCORDING TO RESEARCH COMPILED BY THE HARVARD School for Public Health, nine out of ten people who attempt suicide and survive will not go on to die by suicide at a later date. It is my mother's continued survival, not my father's, that is the statistical anomaly. Nine out of ten women diagnosed with Stage IIIC ovarian cancer do not survive eighteen months. My mother has been in remission for eight years. I don't know what the survival rates are for women with bipolar disorder, closeted gay husbands and Stage IIIC ovarian cancer, but they can't be good.

Had my mother died of ovarian cancer in those first eighteen months, or any time over the next four years, she would have gone to her grave not knowing my father's secret. My father did not want my mother to die of ovarian cancer, but it must have crossed his mind, at least once, that if she did die, he would be free of the burden of keeping his secret. I don't mean to suggest that he hoped for this, for her death from cancer. He would never have hoped for that. But he would have hoped – must have hoped – that the need to keep his secret would someday be gone from the world.

This hope has come to pass.

My mother does not regret knowing. She prefers pain and loneliness to ignorance and deception. But she wishes that she'd known long before, sometime after her children were born, sometime when she would have had more time to live with the truth of things as they were. But in life, as in cards, my mother is a purist. She scorns, she derides – she will not play – those soft games where you pass cards left or right, dumping the cards you need least. You play the hand you're dealt.

Two Different Stories

I CAME INTO OUR BEDROOM ONE SUNDAY AFTERNOON. I forget what I was doing. Maybe I was carrying a basket of laundry. Christine doesn't fold or put away laundry. That's not her department. Oliver was sitting on our bed reading a magazine. He looked pale and troubled. He looked up at me and said, "I don't understand."

He showed me the magazine, published a year earlier. The October 2008 issue of *The Sun* was open to an essay written by an author named Gregory Martin. The title of the essay was "The Family Plot."

OLIVER DID NOT look sad so much as confused. The magazine had been in the magazine rack beside my bed, in the back, behind other literary magazines. I didn't know that Oliver looked through the magazines in my magazine bin.

Oliver said, "Did Grandpa attempt suicide?"

Oliver knew about suicide. He knew about hara-kiri, the ritual suicide by self-disembowelment on a sword, practiced by samurai in traditional Japanese culture. He knew about Japanese kamikaze pilots in World War II who flew their planes into American ships.

I could feel my heart thumping in my chest. I didn't know what to say, so I said, "Yes. Grandpa did attempt suicide. It happened three summers ago."

I sat down beside Oliver on the bed. I put my hand on his shoulder. I asked him how much of the essay he had read.

He said, "Not very much. Why were you in that graveyard?"

I said, "I don't really know. I guess because I was so sad."

I took the magazine from his hands. Then I said, "I'm going to get Mommy. Okay? I'll be right back."

Oliver said, "Okay."

Christine was in the living room. I can't remember what she was doing and neither can she. I held up the magazine. I said, "Oliver was reading this."

"Goddamn," she said. She looked scared.

We went back into the bedroom together. Oliver was still sitting on the bed, his legs crossed. Christine and I stood near him. I was waiting for Christine to say something first. But she didn't say anything for a long time. Oliver had that look on his face that meant that he thought he was in trouble.

Christine sighed.

"It's okay, son," I said.

Christine said, "I'm so sorry, Oliver. I wish you didn't know. You're not old enough. That essay is for adults. That magazine should not have been out." She turned and shot me a look even though she knew it was there as well as I did.

Oliver said, "Why did Grandpa try to kill himself?"

I said, "Grandpa was terribly sad when he realized he and Granny were going to get a divorce."

Oliver nodded. "But how? How did Grandpa try to kill himself?"

"He took too much medicine," Christine said. She sat down on the bed next to Oliver. She put her forehead on his forehead. She put her hand on the back of Oliver's head and held it there. She let go and looked him in the eye. "He took lots and lots of medicine, and so his body tried to shut down. He made a terrible mistake. His brain wasn't working well because of his sadness."

Oliver put his elbows to his knees and his chin in his hands.

Christine said, "Oh, sweetheart, I wish you hadn't found out this way."

"It's not your fault, Oliver," I said. "It's our fault. It's my fault."

Christine said, "This is not a secret, but Evan is not old enough to know this. Do you understand?"

Oliver said, "I won't tell him."

"Mommy and Daddy will tell him when he's older," I said.

I don't remember what else we said. I don't remember if Oliver asked more questions that we weren't willing to answer. I don't think he did. I think he became quiet and serious. Maybe he was puzzling over events in his memory, looking for clues. I don't remember if the three of us stayed there on the bed for awhile before leaving the room one by one, or if Christine left first and fumed somewhere, and I stayed with Oliver for a few minutes longer. I don't remember where Evan was when this happened, except that he was not there.

That night, after the boys were asleep, Christine and I were in bed, and she turned to me. "We can tell the boys that Grandpa is gay, and we will. They should know that. But there are things you keep from children. I hate that Oliver knows his Grandpa tried to kill himself. That he even knows it's a possibility. It's almost worse that it was an attempt. Go ahead, when you're sad, try to kill yourself, but you'll live to tell about it and be happy again. Everything can turn out okay. I hate that Oliver knows that. We should have known better. Everybody knows better. That's our mistake. Every kid knows what's in their parents' nightstand. I know I did."

I didn't know how to feel. But I trusted Christine's conviction more than my confusion. I lacked Christine's conviction and clarity because I wanted so badly to unburden myself. I wanted to release the pressure of my own silence. But that was not what my children needed. There was a difference between the story my children needed to hear and the story I needed to tell them. Those were two different stories.

Secret Talent

BENEDICT CAREY WROTE IN *THE NEW YORK TIMES*, "Psychologists have long considered the ability to keep secrets as central to healthy development. Children as young as six or seven learn to stay quiet about their mother's birthday present." Carey quotes Daniel Wegner, the white bear psychology professor, who says, "In a very deep sense, you don't have a self unless you have a secret ... And we are now learning that some people are better at doing this than others."

Ice Cream

EVAN WANDERS THE FIELD. THE SOCCER BALL HAS NO magnetic attraction on his imagination or desire. When it rolls near him, he regards it with only mild curiosity. I sometimes feel as if Evan has been sent to earth to administer me a Zen lesson on the dangers of the desire to compete, to win, to dominate one's opponent.

I'm Oliver's soccer coach but not Evan's. It's too difficult for scheduling – with all the games and practices – for me to coach both boys' teams. So I'm the referee when Evan's team, the Poison Geckos, are the home team. Evan's coach is a good guy, competitive, fun. His son's a ringer, the best player on the team, not that this matters. One day at practice Evan ran around hugging his teammates instead of kicking the ball. A few of Evan's teammates greeted his affection warmly and returned it. Other teammates were impeded from kicking the ball and scoring goals. I intervened. Evan stopped hugging. He ran around and sang a song instead.

When I returned to the sidelines where I belonged, another father, my neighbor Andrew, whose son was sometimes also yellow-carded for hugging, suggested that the two of us start a support group.

"Do I look murderous?"

"We have to take the long view," he said.

On the drive home from practice, I told Evan that he needed to try harder. When it was time to play soccer, you played soccer.

He could hug his friends some other time. He could wander around and sing to himself at recess or at home.

"You've got to try to kick the ball," I said.

"But the other kids are so much better than I am," he said.

"They're not that much better," I said. "They might not even be better at all. They're just watching the ball and trying to kick it. Will you try to watch the ball?"

"Okay, Dad." He had tears in his eyes.

"Hey, Evan."

He didn't answer.

"It's okay. I want you to have fun. And you had fun today, didn't you?"

Evan looked out the window. It was getting dark. He was probably hungry and dinner must have seemed a long way off.

That night, Evan was constipated. He called out from the toilet. "I need some FIBER!" So Christine mixed him an orange Metamucil highball, which I can't even look at without my stomach turning. She sat down on the green tile floor and handed it to Evan as he sat naked on the toilet. He thanked her. He drank it. He gave her back the empty glass. He said, "I don't want to play soccer next year. I don't want to let my teammates down." I hadn't said this to him, that he was letting his teammates down. Maybe I had. Inside the bathroom, Christine was saying nurturing things. They were in there a long time. What was wrong with me? Why did I care so much that Evan be competitive? Some games, Evan didn't make a single attempt to kick the ball, especially if it was a hot day. At his best, he ran alongside the herd. He was the one the wolves had their eye on.

That night I couldn't sleep. I stayed up thinking about my father, who came to all my games when I was growing up. I played soccer, baseball, basketball, football, and ran track. I was crazy about sports as a kid and as a teenager and, well, pretty much now. I can't teach an 11:00 a.m. class because it interferes with my stretching and warm-up before the noon basketball game at the university gym. When I was a boy, my father sat in the middle

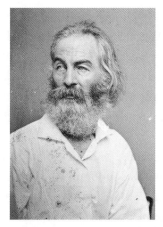

of the stands where I could see him. He was always supportive; he never once pressured me. I pressured myself plenty all on my own. My father cared if I won or lost but only because I cared so much. Otherwise he was calm and gentle in a way that I was not, not ever, not when it came to sports.

Sometime past midnight, I sat up in bed. The room was in shadow. A number of questions came to me in rapid succession. Why couldn't Evan hug his teammates if he wanted to? Why was I so embarrassed? What was that all about? Was it really because he was interrupting practice? Distracting the other players? Why so angry? Disappointed? Was my disappointment really about his attention span? Did it really have anything to do with sports? A hug from a six-year-old was a hug. It was affection and happiness and innocence. It was beautiful. I was the ugly one with the scowl on my face. Where was my sense of humor? Where was my joy in my son's easy authenticity? Why was I disappointed that my son didn't want to be the most dominant six-year-old boy on the field? What the fuck was wrong with me? What would Walt Whitman say? He would sound his barbaric yawp right in my face.

I got up and went into the kitchen and opened Christine's stainless steel refrigerator. A swath of light streamed into the dark. I poured myself a glass of milk. Why did it seem that my epiphanic, revelatory thoughts on this matter were not particularly new or profound? Why was I so stupid? Hadn't I learned anything?

ALL SEASON LONG, I'd told Evan, that if he kicked the ball five times in a game, I'd take him out for ice cream. He'd never earned ice cream. Late in the first half of the last game of the fall season, the ball rolled right at him. He noticed it. He didn't have to move anything but the muscles in his lower right leg. He moved them. He made contact, small black cleat on ball. He kicked the ball with his toe, not his instep or laces, but still. The ball rolled away from Evan in the wrong direction, toward the other team's goal. Evan was ecstatic. I was on the field, refereeing. I saw it all.

Evan abandoned the ball, ran toward me and shouted, "Dad! I kicked it! That's one!"

"Awesome," I whispered neutrally. "Kick it again." I felt guilty that this longstanding bribe was suddenly working, especially after my late-night epiphany. I didn't want Evan to play soccer just to please me. But I was pleased, despite myself. Soccer was such a great game. I'd thought all along that if he just got into it, he might start to like it for its own sake.

In the second half, a boy on Evan's team took a well-kicked ball in the stomach and had the wind knocked out of him. I blew the whistle, stopped play and had everyone take a knee. The boy moaned but didn't cry. He stood up quickly but was still doubled over. He was trying to shake it off. He didn't look over to the sidelines. The last thing this boy wanted was what he really wanted: a hug from his mom or dad. I put my hand on his shoulder. I asked him if he wanted to take a break for a while. He could come back in whenever he was ready. He winced. He shook his head. He didn't want to go out. I told him to tell me when he was ready. He took a few breaths and stood up straight. He was ready.

The re-start in this situation is a drop ball. Two players face off and the referee drops the ball between them and when it hits the ground, the ball is live. There had been a number of drop ball re-starts. The usual suspects volunteered, raising their hands highly. Evan didn't raise his hand, but I chose him anyway. Then I chose the one boy on the other team who was a butterfly chaser like Evan. They faced each other. I held the ball between them.

"Now when the ball hits the ground, you guys kick it, okay?" They nodded.

I dropped the ball. Evan got to it first and kicked it hard. The ball ricocheted off the other boy's shin guard and came back to Evan. He kicked the ball again. It ricocheted back. Evan kicked it again and the ball rolled clear.

"Dad!" Evan screamed. "That makes four!"

"I know," I said out of the side of my mouth. "Go get one more."

Six-year-olds in Evan's league play twenty minute halves. With four minutes left in the second half, it didn't look like Evan was going to get his fifth kick. He wasn't watching the ball but walking around in loose circles near the middle of the field. After the last game, which his team had lost twelve to three, Evan asked me, "Did we win?"

The ball rolled toward Evan. Something registered in his peripheral vision. He looked up. There wasn't enough time for conscious thought. It would have to be all reflex. Evan's primal instincts kicked the ball. The ball went rolling forward, in the right direction. There was no one between the ball and the goal. But the goal was a long way off and Evan hadn't kicked it that hard. He would have to run after it and kick it again to score. He would probably have to kick it a few times.

Evan turned and ran away from the ball, toward me. "That's five!" He did an ice cream dance.

A boy on the other team reached Evan's ball, turned it skillfully, and took off dribbling in the other direction.

I ran along near the play. Evan ran beside me. He tugged on my black and white jersey. "Dad," he said, as if I had failed to understand the significance of what had happened. "That's five. Ice cream. Remember?"

"Yes, son. I remember. Great job." I stopped and put my hand out and we high-fived, but I felt awful inside, a terrible sinking feeling. Then I ran across the field towards the ball.

Evan veered off, settled into a stroll. He returned to circling the center of the field. Boys ran back and forth, chasing and kicking the ball.

After the game Evan ran happily through the tunnel made by all the parents' upraised, connecting hands. This is Evan's favorite part of the game. He sat on the grass with the other boys and savored his post-game Rice Krispie bar. He drank his juice box. He told everyone – his teammates, their parents – about his ice cream plans and how this reward had come about. There was envy and begging. One teammate mentioned sweetly to his parents that he had kicked the ball a lot more than five times. Another teammate seconded this general estimation to his parents. These parents shook their heads. They kept their thoughts to themselves. Evan was oblivious. He had met the challenge. His work here was done.

Fractions and Story Problems

CHRISTINE CAME HOME FROM GROCERY SHOPPING, AND
I went out to help her bring in the bags. I said, "I want to tell
them. I want to tell them right now."

It was the middle of a Sunday afternoon.

Christine said, "No. I don't think you should."

"I want to."

"They're hungry. It's not a good time."

I said, "There is no good time."

What I didn't say, but what I know now, is that I hated that
Oliver knew only part of the truth about my father. The wrong
part the part we did not want him to know. His Grandpa had
attempted suicide. Sadness over the divorce was only part of the
reason. But Oliver didn't know why they divorced. He didn't
know his grandfather was gay. I thought about him trying to sort
this out in his mind. I thought about how it could not possibly
have made any sense.

So Oliver knew a fraction of what happened and a fraction
of the reason, and Evan knew nothing. This galled me, gnawed
at my conscience. I'd been thinking about it more and more. My
childhood had been one layer of silence and secrets over another.
So had my father's. I did not want to pass on this inheritance to
my sons. I wanted them to know the truth, as much as they could
handle, as much as they were ready for – though I didn't know
how much that was. I wanted them to understand my sadness. I

did not want to be a mystery to my sons – or no more, anyway, than I already was, and always would be.

Christine stood there in the driveway, a gallon jug of milk in each hand.

"I'm telling them," I said.

Christine walked past me, went through the front door and into the kitchen and started putting away groceries. Her jaw was set. She would not make eye contact. We put away all the groceries. She said, "We need to talk to Oliver first."

Oliver was reading a book on the couch. Evan was in the back yard. We asked Oliver if we could talk to him back in the guest bedroom, on the futon. He looked up immediately and said, "Am I in trouble?"

We shook our heads and told him no, at the same time. Oliver said, "I'm definitely in trouble."

We all went back to the futon and sat down.

Christine took Oliver's hands, and said, "Remember that story you read that Daddy wrote, about Grandpa? It was in the magazine next to our bed."

Oliver nodded his head. "When he took all that medicine."

I said, "We're going to tell you more about that story now, but we want to make sure you don't tell Evan about Grandpa taking too much medicine. He's not old enough to know that."

"Suicide," Oliver said.

"He's not old enough to know about that," I said again.

Oliver nodded. "I know."

Christine said, "But we want you to know that you can talk to us about it, if you want. Anytime. We didn't tell you that well enough last time."

Christine waited. Oliver didn't say anything.

I went out to the back yard to get Evan. He was swinging in the hammock that Christine had strung under the treehouse. He was singing to himself. At the time, I didn't think, "He's so happy. This isn't the right time. He's too little." Evan rolled out of the hammock and came running when I called his name and told him we were having a family meeting back on the futon. He ran through our small house and back into the guest bedroom and jumped on Oliver and they started wrestling. Christine and I both pulled them apart, untangling arms and legs. Christine sat between them and tried to keep them apart. Evan lunged for Oliver again.

I pulled up a chair and sat opposite them and said, "We have something to tell you both about why Granny and Grandpa got divorced."

Evan stopped reaching for Oliver. He looked up at me. The play went out of his face.

I didn't know what I was going to say. Even though I'd been thinking for more than two years about what I might say to them someday about this, I hadn't rehearsed anything. I just started talking.

"Granny and Grandpa divorced because Grandpa is gay. But Granny didn't know this about him for years and years because Grandpa kept it a secret. When they got married, forty years ago, she didn't know he was gay. She didn't know when I was growing up, either. Grandpa kept it a secret from her because he grew up in a time when it wasn't okay to be gay. He grew up in a time when you could get beaten up or even killed if you were gay, especially where he lived, in the South. Remember how we talked about the Ku Klux Klan. Well, Grandpa grew up in a time and a place where there were people like the Ku Klux Klan who hated people who were gay and would hurt them terribly."

Oliver said, "The Ku Klux Klan isn't gone. There are still people in the Ku Klux Klan, and they still believe those things."

Christine said, "That's right, Oliver."

Evan shouted, "Grandpa is *gay*?" He started to cry. He jumped off the couch and started running around the room, waving his arms in the air. He shouted, "Too sad. Too sad. I don't want to hear anymore." He ran out of the room.

Before Christine and I could go after him, he ran back in

and I pulled him on to my lap. He shouted, "Does that mean I'm gay? Does that mean I'm a quarter gay?"

"No son, that–"

"But you're *half* gay, Dad!" Evan shouted.

"No, it doesn't–"

"I hate Grandpa. Papa is my favorite now." Evan's thin little chest was heaving.

Christine gave me a look and shook her head. *Why are we doing this?*

Oliver said, "Did Grandpa have affairs?"

"Yes," I said. "He did. He had affairs with men. He was unfaithful to Granny, and that's another reason why they divorced."

Oliver nodded. I had never seen him so serious.

Evan shouted, "Why didn't you tell us? I'm so angry at you for not telling us!"

I said, "I'm sorry I didn't tell you. I didn't think you were old enough."

Evan shouted, "I'm gay! I know it! I'm going to be gay now! Oh no! This is the gay part of me, right here." He started rubbing his left forearm with his right hand. "I knew it. This is the part that's gay."

Christine said, "Sweetheart, just because Grandpa is gay doesn't mean that you will be gay. Daddy's not gay. But if you are gay, that's okay. There's nothing wrong with being gay. Remember, your aunt Momo is gay."

Evan smiled. "And Anne is gay."

"Mom, they're lesbians," Oliver said.

"Yes, they are. That's right. But it's also okay to say that they're gay. And listen, Evan. Joey and Nora, your cousins, their moms are gay. Megan and Mary, they're lesbians. They're gay, too. And Randall, Momo's friend from the bakery. He's gay."

Evan took a deep breath. He wiped his tears from his face with the back of his arm. "I'm mad at Grandpa."

"I'm mad at him, too," I said. "Even now, I'm mad at him."

Not all the time. But I'm still mad. You get to be mad at him. You can even tell him that you're mad. He'll understand."

Evan didn't say anything. We were all quiet for a moment. I took a deep breath myself. I tried to meet Christine's eyes, but she wouldn't take her eyes off the boys. She was studying them. Oliver's lips were pressed together in a line, his brow was furrowed. Later that day he'd tell Christine how often he heard boys at school call other boys "gay," and he didn't like it, but he didn't know what to do. Evan had left my lap and was now sprawled on his back on the futon, his arms and legs in every direction. He was looking at the ceiling.

Christine stood up. She said, "Do you boys want to say anything? Do you have any questions?"

Evan said, "I feel sad for Granny."

"I do, too," I said.

"Does Granny know?" Evan asked.

"She does now," Christine said.

"That's why they got a divorce," Oliver said.

"That's right," I said.

"You should have told us, Dad," Evan said.

I didn't say anything. Christine kissed both boys on the forehead and left the room.

Hay Ride

MY FATHER CAME TO VISIT FOR A LONG WEEKEND, DRIV-
ing seven hours to see us from his home in Arizona. He'd found
a three bedroom house fifteen miles north of Kingman. His house
was literally at the end of the road. The asphalt ended ten feet
beyond his driveway. Across a barbed wire fence was the Mojave
desert.

He knocked softly on the front door close to midnight. The
boys were asleep. Christine and I were in bed. I invited him
inside and hugged him. Then we held each other at arm's length,
and took each other in. All my life, my father had been six feet
tall. I stand five feet ten inches in my basketball shoes. But now
my father was shorter than me. He'd gained a little weight, but
not much. He looked good. I carried his bag into the guest
bedroom, told him I was glad he'd come, and said I'd see him in
the morning. He coughed most of the night, hacking and wheezing.

The next morning, Christine made waffles, cut up bananas
and strawberries, and we all sat around the kitchen table eating
and talking. Oliver and Evan took turns sitting in their Grandpa's
lap. They held his hand. Christine and my father talked easily, as
they have always done. My father regularly told Christine things
he didn't tell me. He'd recently told Christine that the physical
therapist he was seeing for back pain, a twenty-four-year-old
man, was a "dreamboat."

This morning, Christine and my father talked about their
work, about the days when there are just too many patients.

They talked about all the time they spend on their feet and the need for good orthotics. They talked about medication errors. My father told the story of the time when my brother was only ten months old, before I was born. My brother had such a high fever that he kept having febrile seizures and the doctors packed him in ice. My father talked about how helpless he felt, how worried he was. Christine talked about the time when Evan was a baby and was breathing way too fast. He was in and out of the pediatric ER for almost ten weeks.

"I think my greatest fear during that time," Christine said, "was that I'd never get to know him. I was never carefree. I only saw the problem. I didn't enjoy Evan as a baby, not nearly enough."

Evan was staring at Christine, his eyes wide. I was staring at my father.

My father said, "I know exactly what you mean."

Then he and Christine talked about the shopping trip the two of them had planned for the afternoon. My father wanted to find drapes for his new house and wanted Christine's advice and her company. I didn't say anything about him vying to become Christine's trendy, token sitcom gay best friend. I could recognize my petulant, sarcastic thoughts, even if I couldn't stop them from registering. Then I recognized what I was really feeling. Jealousy. My father was at ease with Christine in a way that he never was with me.

I cleared the table and washed dishes. The kitchen was spotless.

The morning passed and no one mentioned suicide attempts. No one mentioned sexual orientation. There was no mention of divorce or loneliness. No one mentioned that it seemed as if, with this move to Arizona, my father had gone right back in the closet. No one at his work, at the grocery store, in his neighborhood, knows that he is gay.

But it came to me that morning that the most difficult truths I'd had to accept were not related to my father's homosexuality or what had been done to him as a child. It was far more difficult to accept his loneliness and isolation. And my mother's loneliness and isolation. I had always thought of them together; I had always thought of them comforting one another into their old age. Then, when one of them died, the other would be comforted by the memories of their life together. But those memories were no comfort now.

My father's cell phone rang and he stepped outside on the back porch and took the call. When he came back, he said, "Edna has terminal lung cancer. They're going to put her on hospice." He looked stunned. Christine went over and hugged him. He sat down at the table. Since his divorce, his sister Edna had been his confidant, his best friend. After his suicide attempt, he called and told her everything. She'd known him since the day he was born, but now she knew that he was gay. Now she knew that their father had molested him for years. She loved and accepted him unconditionally, despite her conservative, Southern worldview. He had been to visit her many times in the past two years.

My father talked about the minor back surgery Edna had gone in for. How she had no idea at all about the cancer. But now it had spread all through her body. She didn't have much time left. My father said that he hoped that she would go quickly. He hoped that she wouldn't suffer long.

He said, "It just isn't fair."

I was making another pot of coffee. I said, "You smoke all your life, you're going to get lung cancer."

My father did not look up, but he said, "That's not nice."

Christine shot me a look and shook her head.

"You're right," I said. "I'm sorry."

WE DROVE FORTY-FIVE minutes across the high desert east of Albuquerque to McCall's Pumpkin Patch. My father drove. He had XM Satellite Radio in his car, and we listened to Bill Staines sing "Roseville Fair." We listened to Joan Baez and also Suzanne Vega and Robert Earl Keen, Jr. Sometimes my father sang along.

CHAD MITCHELL TRIO   MCA

We listened to the Chad Mitchell Trio sing "Which Hat Shall I Wear." My father said, "These guys are still touring, after all these years."

We pulled off the interstate and stopped at the stop sign at the top of the ramp. A semi was about thirty yards away, barreling down the lane we needed to cross before turning left onto a rural highway.

I said, "You're going to want to wait. Precious cargo, you know." I meant Oliver and Evan, strapped in the back seat.

My father looked over at me, his head tilted down slightly, taking me in through the top lenses of his bifocals. He said, "I know. My son is in the car."

It was a clear, sunny New Mexico fall day. McCall's Pumpkin Patch is a lot like the Roseville Fair in Bill Staines's song. Wholesome fun. The boys ran through the Corn Maze, a sixteen-acre labyrinth of corn stalks. They shot corn cobs from long rubber slingshots. They jumped on the jumping pillow. They did repeats down the dark, cavernous tunnel slide. They fed goats. They watched as pumpkins exploded from a cannon. The man in the cowboy hat pulled the lever, the cannon fired, and out its long barrel the pumpkin flew so high in the air, and so far, that it landed nearly out of sight. You could see the little puff of dust rise when the pumpkin hit the ground, but you couldn't hear the sound of the impact or see the orange fragments scatter. It was too far away.

We ate chili cheese dogs and french fries. The boys wanted to stay past dark and enter the Haunted Farm, but we told them they weren't old enough, and they didn't argue. The sun was going down. We took a hay ride out to the pumpkin patch, and we each wandered the field searching for the best one. We rode the wagon back, our pumpkins in our lap. My father pulled a huge bag of popcorn out of his backpack and we all took turns plunging our hand inside the bag. I felt uncautiously, unguardedly happy.

We drove back to Albuquerque, listening to more folk music. Patty Griffin sang "Useless Desires." Bob Dylan sang, "Don't Think Twice, It's All Right."

LATER THAT NIGHT, after the boys were in their pajamas and had brushed their teeth, Oliver and I read *Harry Potter and the Order of the Phoenix* on the couch in the living room, and Evan got to read with Grandpa back in the guest bedroom, on the futon, which was folded out to make a bed. They propped up pillows, and Evan read *See Pip Point* to my father, and then my father read to Evan *Henry and Mudge and The Big Test*, a chapter book about Henry and his big dog Mudge's adventures at obedience school.

When I turned off the lamp beside my bed that night, light was still shining out beneath the crack of the closed door of the guest bedroom. My father was awake, reading. He would be up for hours. I did not hold this against him. Two days later he would fly to Georgia to be with Edna, to tell her that he loved her and to say goodbye. A week later, he'd fly back to Georgia again to attend her funeral.

THOSE FOUR DAYS of my father's visit to my home, I didn't know what else there was that I wanted from him, or for him. But I know better now. I want to free him from the burden of my judgment. He has had enough burdens for one lifetime.

A New Commercial

THE BOYS AND I WERE WATCHING THE NBA PLAYOFFS when a commercial came on. (The boys like the commercials way more than the games, and so I'm forbidden to mute them or change the channel.) The commercial was for Google Chrome, but it was also about the It Gets Better Project, the internet video project started by Dan Savage, which provides a forum for gay, lesbian and transgendered people, young and old, to tell their stories, and to urge gay and lesbian teenagers that, however compelled they are to turn to suicide, they need to get through it; they need to choose to live. We'd never seen this commercial before. We thought we had all the NBA Playoffs commercials memorized. I'd never seen a commercial like this in my life. Evan stood up on the couch and started pointing at the TV and shouting "Hey! Look!" I didn't tell him to sit down. Then he was jumping up and down. He was eight years old. Four years had passed since my father had tried to take his life – though Evan still didn't know about that. Or maybe he did. Maybe he knew more than his parents had told him. But he knew his grandfather was gay. And he knew that it was hard to be gay, and this commercial was about how hard it was. This commercial was about his grandfather and for his grandfather. Evan got it. I could see it in his eyes. They were shining. Evan shouted at the screen, "Grandpa needs to see this. We need to call him."

Oliver shouted, "I can't hear. I can't hear what they're saying."

But Evan wouldn't stop, he said, "Listen. It gets better. We need to call Grandpa. He needs to know that."

He kept saying this long after the game came back on. He kept saying this until I called his grandfather and handed Evan the phone.

Flight

MY FATHER IS THOUSANDS OF FEET ABOVE THE EARTH.
He's flying. He's in a small plane over the Arizona desert with
another man who works with him at the nursing home. The man
is an occupational therapist; he owns a Cessna. My father has
never flown in a Cessna before. They're flying from a small
airfield outside Kingman to the resort community of Sedona. It's
early morning. They pass over several mountain ranges. They
land. They have breakfast at the restaurant in the airport. They
fly back.

I don't know what they talk about in the air or on the
ground. I don't know what this man knows or doesn't know about
my father. My guess is this man knows only that my father is
divorced, has grown children and grandchildren, and has moved
to Arizona recently to start another life. I think my father would
tell me if this man has become a lover – though he wouldn't use
that phrase. Or he would tell Christine. Not long before he
moved, my father briefly dated a much younger man. It ended
badly, because this man lied to him. My father was still angry,
weeks later, about being lied to. He felt deeply wronged. He didn't
tell me what the lie was. When I pointed out the irony – that he
was mad about being lied to – my father laughed out loud.

"Yes. You're right," he said. "That is ironic. It hadn't
occurred to me."

I don't know what my father sees from the plane. I don't
know if the morning light is clear and bright so that he can see

the distinguishing features of the landscape – cactus of all kinds, mesas, rock formations reminiscent of Wile E. Coyote and his lifelong, futile pursuit of Road Runner. Or if the distance seems hazy and indistinct. I imagine the trip for him is a welcome release from loneliness. But I don't know if it is strained and awkward due to unspoken longing, or if it is purely friendly, platonic – two men flying together in a small plane. I don't know if my father sees in the desert below a reflection of his inner life, or if he is happy, content, and the rush of take-off and flight has him brimming with hope in the future. I only know what he tells me on the phone, later that day. I am sort-of-happy for him – a happiness mixed with heartache that I don't have a name for but am learning to accept. I am surrendering to him his life. His life is not mine to have or to hold, and never has been.

Epilogue

I STILL MARK THE BEGINNING OF MY NEW RELATIONSHIP with my father from that suicide attempt. But now I have to ask myself: how long has it been? And I have to do the math. It has been four and a half years. I'll never completely separate the truth of who my father is from the shock of that phone call, from that awful mystery of knowing he had tried to take his life but not knowing why.

But I know now, and I know enough. If my father is more of a mystery to me now than he ever was before, it's because I know and love him more, not less. My father did not think this was possible; he did not think his children could bear the truth of who he was and still love him. He did not think he could bear the truth, himself. He could not imagine the future in which we are all living now. How could he have? Who can?

I don't know now whether anyone at my father's work or in his life in Arizona knows that he is gay. I don't need to know. I've stopped asking. If he wants to tell me, he will. I know that next summer he plans to drive up the west coast, to Anthony's Home Court, in Long Beach, Washington, which is not a typical RV park – far from it. I'm hoping that Christine and I and Oliver and Evan can meet him there, rent a big cabin for four or five days. I've been thinking about asking him about this, but I haven't yet figured out how. But I will.

A few weeks ago I emailed him to see if he wanted to come for Thanksgiving. Here's his reply:

Subject: **RE: Thanksgiving**

Date: Sun, 13 Nov 2011

Thanks so much for the invitation. I do appreciate the thought.

My friend, Mary, another speech therapist, and I are hosting a Thanks-giving dinner at my house for two of her friends and one of the physical therapists who's a Traveler and has no time to get home with family for just one day. It will be the first time I've actually entertained in my house and I'm really looking forward to it.

But we can think about next year.

Love you a ton,

Dad

Acknowledgements

THANKS TO MY FATHER, FOR GIVING HIMSELF AND HIS story to these pages. Thanks to my mother, for her grit, her humor, her many readings of this book, and her lifelong encouragement of my writing. Thanks to Chris Martin, Eric Puchner, Dan Stolar, Andrea Hollander Budy, Mark Sundeen, and Bill Fanning, for their careful reading of early drafts, and for their friendship and encouragement. Thanks to Doug Stewart at Sterling Lord Literistic. Thanks to the editors at *The Sun* magazine, for publishing the essay "The Family Plot, " which grew into this book. At Hawthorne Books, thanks to Liz Crain, Adam O'Connor Rodriguez, and especially Rhonda Hughes, for her belief in this story and her editorial insight. Thanks again, and always, to my wife, Christine.